relit

How to Rekindle Yourself in the Darkness of Compassion Fatigue

Edited by
Peter Dudley and
Antoinette LeCouteur

Copyright © 2024 by Gray Bear Publications
All Rights Reserved
No part of this book may be reproduced or retransmitted in any form or by any means, electronic or mechanical, without written permission of the publisher. Authors retain full rights to their own contributions.

Requests and inquiries may be sent to info@graybearpublications.com. Authors are generally available for speaking, interviews, and events.

Edited by Peter Dudley
Cover Art by Peter Dudley
Headshot photography provided by the authors.
Non-headshot photographs by Antoinette LeCouteur
Published by Gray Bear Publications, an imprint of Gray Bear Coaching, LLC
graybearpublications.com

ISBN: 979-8-9876637-6-9
Also available in paperback and ebook

Dedication

For all those who feel called to care for others, and who follow that call with all their heart and soul.

Contents

Introduction: *A Beacon of Hope When Darkness Falls* .... *i*

Allison K. Wyman, JD, MPA
Your Future is Far More Beautiful Than You Could Ever Imagine 5

Margaret Stauffer, MS, LMFT
When Professional and Personal Collide 19

Larry Brouder
How to Strengthen Your Compassionate Self 29

Faith Albright, DVM
Love is Never Wasted 43

Jean C. Accius, Ph.D.
Rising Above: A Journey of Loss, Resilience, and the Fight for Equity and Justice 59

Sally Spencer-Thomas, Psy.D.
Supporting a Loved One With Mental Health Challenges 73

Richa Chadha, MBA, MS
From Duty to Choice: Navigating Cultural Expectations 95

Antoinette LeCouteur
When She is Gone, We Will Still be a Family 111

Tammy Hurst, RN, MSN, NC-BC
The Truth from a Bedside Nurse 127

Peter Dudley, PCC
Show up. Try hard. Be nice. 137

Jill Louise Léger
Recreation Therapy & Me: Compassion Fatigue In Elder Care 151
Rereation Therapy 101 169

Dr. Kenya Oscar Radoli
Nurturing Resilience: Practical Strategies for Organization Change Leaders 181

Laura Plato, MSc
Nature's Nurture: Nature Connection in Caregiver Well-Being 199

Nayely Duran, ACC
Embracing Compassion Without Losing Yourself 221

Dennis Brozzo, PMP
On Love, Loss, and Recovery from Devastation 239

Catherine Krause, RN, PHN and Jerry Krause, Ph.D.
Lessening Compassion Fatigue Through an Empowerment Approach 259

Photographs and Poems

Photographs

Tea Light Candles 16
Melted Rainbow Ice Cream 17
Buttercups with Cemetery Behind 40
Cat in Window 41
Ginkgo Leaves After a Rain 57
Cherry Blossoms on a Clear Day 71
Snowy Egret Takes Flight 93
Hello, Sunflower 109
Marigolds on a Ledge 123
A Bench in the City 124
Ernie's Pond 125
A Faucet in Black and White 135
Rainbow Umbrella 149
Sunflower with Blue Sky 168
Creeping Chameleon 179
Lights on a City Wall 197
Way Out 219
A Crutch on the Sidewalk 237
Committed 255
Poppies Along a Path 256
Sailing Onward 280

Poems

Weightless 17
Waiting 40
A Child's Wish 124
Finding Contentment 256

Introduction

A Beacon of Hope When Darkness Falls

Caring is one of the most human and natural things there is. It's also exhausting. That exhaustion breaks people, but it doesn't have to.

Millions of people go into heart-based roles every year because they care about something. Some choose it as a profession, from nursing to veterinary medicine to law to life coaching. Millions are thrust into unpaid caregiving roles due to a loved one's illness, the natural aging process their parents are going through, or another kind of crisis like a grandchild's sudden need for a guardian.

The amount of caring that goes on every day astounds and inspires us. The amount of burnout and compassion fatigue all that caring creates is devastating, both individually and to society as a whole.

Compassion fatigue—the physical and mental exhaustion and detachment experienced by those who care—is a growing yet largely unrecognized and undiscussed concern. It can be caused by many different factors, such as systemic inequities, a feeling of powerlessness, the ingratitude of those being helped, and just plain old overwhelm. It can also take many forms, from profound exhaustion to detachment to a loss of the ability to feel joy.

Every time a mid-career woman is forced to drop out of the workforce to care for an aging parent, society suffers. Every time a nurse or teacher quits due to burnout, society suffers. Every time a family falls apart because of the strife, conflict, and financial distress caused by caregiving, society suffers.

Our personal and professional experiences exposed us to a world where people in caring roles are starving for practical, useful, actionable help. We've interacted with hundreds of individuals who feel not just the profound exhaustion of compassion fatigue, but also a heavy sense of isolation and shame because of it. When you're in a caring role, it's almost impossible to admit out loud how hard it is, and how sometimes you feel like you just can't go on anymore.

Apart from a few scholarly articles and a handful of books about caregiver burnout, we saw a distressing lack of relevant, insightful, and actionable information on how to deal with it.

That's why we decided to create this book.

Each of the experts contributing their wisdom has experienced compassion fatigue and overcome it. Each has a moving personal story that is both unique and very relatable on a human level. We sought out people with a variety of stories and backgrounds, in different professions, and with different experiences of compassion fatigue.

Introduction: A Beacon of Hope When Darkness Falls

You'll find something valuable in every chapter. You can start anywhere, dip in and out of the book again and again, and still take away more with each read. That's been our experience compiling and editing this book.

We decided to call this book *relit* because every story is one of resilience. Each is a story of a caring person who has felt on the verge of being extinguished, but who found ways to rekindle their spirit. Some found help. Some found it within themselves. Some found it within nature, or family, or self-care techniques. Every one decided to share what they learned along the way so that others may learn how to prepare for what is to come, and so that others may have a light to follow in the darkest moments.

We sincerely hope this book will be that beacon for you, and for thousands of others who heed the call to care.

About the Photography

Author photos were provided by the authors. The other photographs included throughout the book were taken by Antoinette LeCouteur. They symbolize the range of feelings people experience through burnout and resilience and are not intended to accompany or illustrate the text of any particular chapter.

About the Poetry

The poems that appear between chapters were written by Peter Dudley and selected from his personal archive of previously unpublished poetry.

Allison K. Wyman, JD, MPA

Allison is an attorney who specializes in family caregiving, wills, trusts, estates, and healthcare. As a two-time cancer caregiver to her parents, Allison opened The Law Office of Allison K. Wyman because she understands the heaviness and confusion that accompany family caregiving, and she seeks to support families by providing legal explanations and tailored practical solutions. Allison holds a law degree from Georgetown University Law Center, and a Master of Public Administration from the Maxwell School of Citizenship and Public Affairs. In addition to law, Allison offers a monthly membership that helps caregivers begin their day in joy and end their day in peace, VIP days for families serious about preparing for caregiving, and a podcast, the Cozy Caregiver Café, available on Apple and Spotify! Learn more about all these heart-centered offerings at cozycaregivercafe.com.

Allison K. Wyman, JD, MPA

Your Future is Far More Beautiful Than You Could Ever Imagine

Fall: The Best "No" I Ever Received

My Dad died six months before my wedding, so I walked myself down the aisle.

As a freshman in college, I visited New York City and decided that was the place I had to live. So I applied to transfer colleges from a Boston school that was an hour away from my hometown in New Hampshire, to a school in New York City. As I waited for Decision Day, I visualized my life in the future and wrote down three statements I saw as DONE:

1. I am married to Dan.
2. We live in New York City where I practice law.
3. We have one child when I am 34–36 years old.

This was my future.

I can still remember opening the email with my admission decision, so sure I was supposed to live in New York City and this was my ticket there. Then I saw the words "We regret to inform you…"

My Dad sent me flowers with a short note that read, "I love you and I'm so proud of you." This was a phrase he repeated all the time through notes left on the kitchen counter in his signature CAPS LOCK WRITING, always ending in "Love, Dad." If my childhood was the shape of a constellation, each nub would be one of these notes; words that applied differently yet equally to celebrate the highs and sit with the lows.

I knew I was supposed to live in New York City with a certainty that felt at home in my body in the same way as when I began dating my husband. So, aside from my college rejection, I also felt… embarrassed. I had a big dream—a huge vision for my life beyond a specific college and major—that I had put out into the world. And the world had rejected it.

Or so it seemed.

I know now God's protections sometimes come in the form of rejections.

Less than a year later, my Dad was diagnosed with cancer. He received treatment and had surgery right there in Boston, mere minutes from my dorm room. I spent most weekends in New Hampshire, conveniently taking a bus that left on the hour from South Station directly to my hometown. And I was in his room at the Hospice House when he died.

That time with him and my mom, and my then-boyfriend-now-husband, Dan, was everything.

Is everything.

And I don't know how it would have happened if I'd been far away at a college in New York City.

That rejection was the best "no" I've ever received.

But, in caregiving, sometimes the end is where the story really begins…

Winter, Part I: The Rules of Compassion Fatigue

After my Dad died, I turned cold. It's almost like to honor that December day he died, my saddest day, my body took a snapshot and then stayed like that to preserve it.

I didn't drink or do drugs; I was already numb.

Looking back, I now realize what I truly was: *Tired.*

Tired as in a deep, heavy exhaustion, the kind that can only come after something ends, but which is itself an event where the beginning and end, seemingly billowing and fluid, become welded together—an art-installation gone wrong.

With no way out.

After caregiving, caregivers need rest. This may seem obvious, but it's actually not in practice, so I'm going to repeat this sentence.

After caregiving, caregivers need rest.

And by rest, I mean deep rest. This is not a good night's sleep, or a day away, or even a get-away that's distracting in the best-way, with action-packed adventures. I mean no responsibilities, no pressure, for as long as someone needs to heal.

The problem is, of course, that life doesn't work like this.

After caregiving we have relationships we've neglected, jobs where we've slipped—the river has kept flowing, and now that we're on the river again, we must quickly learn our new environment.

This learning process can be entertaining, but it's also exhausting. And when you take a caregiver who has given everything of themselves, there's simply no energy to start fresh.

The energy is gone.

That version of you is gone.

Compassion fatigue shows up in many ways. I think it's a natural part of caregiving—one we needn't be ashamed of, but it's a slick and slippery visitor that can quickly become an unwelcome guest.

For me, compassion fatigue made me numb and disinterested. I simply didn't care anymore.

But since truly caring about people is my superpower, I lost a huge part of what made me, me.

And a few years later God called me again to care for someone I love.

Winter, Part II

It sometimes doesn't seem fair that Winter stays and stays, but it has, and it does, and it will.

My winter grew longer when, in 2013, my mom was diagnosed with cancer. At that point my Dad had been gone for six years, my mom hadn't remarried, and as an only child I didn't want her to go through this alone.

Have you ever thought back on a memory and realized your body is reliving it, like it's happening right now, even though your mind knows it's something from the past? When I think now about receiving that call about my mom's cancer diagnosis, my body still goes back.

In fact, it's going back right now.

As I write this, I can feel the tension in my neck. Shallow breathing. Mouth quivering. And now I'm starting to cry. And this is from something that happened 11 years ago. Something that's over. Where the outcome is good—my mom is healthy and still here.

I share this because if you're a former caregiver and you don't understand why you still feel like you're in caregiving, it's because that feeling never truly leaves you. How can it? The combination of someone you love deeply with receipt of terrifying news is not something you forget. But even though it will be a part of your body forever, there's a way for it to be a passenger in your big bus of memories and emotions, while never the driver.

I was sitting at my desk, three weeks into my dream job at my dream law firm, when my phone rang. It wasn't a number I recognized.

"Hello," I said.

"Is this Allison?" the voice answered back.

"Yes…" I responded, thinking someone was about to try to sell me something.

"This is your mom's doctor. She's still asleep, but she just had a colonoscopy. She has cancer, and you should come home now."

I can't remember how the conversation ended, and I can't remember how I made it to New Hampshire. I think I flew home, Washington, DC to New Hampshire, but those memories are elusive, spinning, and gone. I can't remember who picked me up, or where. I can't remember the moment I saw my mom.

I think it's our cat, Leo, who tethers me to this memory, because I knew he had to be cared for while I was in New Hampshire.

I also remember packing up my home and my whole life in DC when I decided to move back to New Hampshire for the year. We had recently bought our first home, a condo on Capitol Hill, and the life I envisioned and felt so excited about was now scattered, a scrapbook page torn up and strewn about, blown by the wind in all directions, never to be whole again.

Months later, when an acquaintance moved into our home in DC to watch it for the year, I wrote this poem after she excitedly texted me about hanging new curtains.

> *Someone is hanging curtains in my home.*
> *But it isn't me.*
> *I lived there*
> *I lived there*
> *I swear it was me!*
> *At least I think it was…*
> *but maybe…*
> *it was just a dream*

Staying with my mom for that year is something I'm deeply proud of. But it was also incredibly hard. The physical acts of caregiving were manageable, but the emotional elements were very, very heavy.

In the evenings, when I'd sit against my headboard in my childhood twin bed, door ajar just in case my mom needed me or something happened, covered by a blanket for comfort more than warmth, I'd think about the day and what the day could have been like had I been living my life in Washington, DC. This dreaming, which served as an escape, helped me exist in a life I felt knocked into, one where my mom was buying me groceries and I drove a borrowed car.

In January, three months into caring for my mom, I attended my swearing-in ceremony to officially become a licensed attorney in New York. My mom and I went together; she saw it as a fun getaway in Albany, but I dreaded seeing my friends and colleagues—yet another reminder of the life I wasn't living. My mom stayed up late that night enjoying herself in the hotel's restaurant, and I turned in early and cried myself to sleep.

Now, at this point, you may be thinking I seem like a spoiled brat. My mom was fighting cancer, for God's sake! How could I possibly think about my career and the life I was missing? Boo-hoo, Allison! Reality check: it's not about you!

The truth is, I was grateful. To this day, I'm still grateful that I took that year to care for my mom. That I could hold her hand through the experience and show up for her with the principles and heart she instilled in me.

And if you're caregiving, and you're reading this and nodding, I also know you are grateful for the role you have in caring for the person you love. Of course you are. But that role comes with a price, and that price is often the vision and realities of a life that moments ago was so real and now appears hazy in the distance.

One element of compassion fatigue that needs more attention is the energy we lose when our lives change so dramatically. There's the giving of care and attention to the person we love, and that can be both sustaining and draining. But what about the level of the reservoir beforehand? My reservoir dropped dramatically when I fell into another version of my life. I gave everything I had to my mom, but simply put, I started with less to give.

Winter, Part III

I like rules. In hindsight, I wished someone had explained the rules of caregiving and compassion fatigue to me. Then I would have understood that instead of feeling like I was lost in the wilderness, I was simply on a well-trodden path, in good company with millions of caregivers who had walked before me.

The rules are quite simple:

In caregiving, you end up giving all that you have, for as long as you can.

Even after all that effort, you still may not find yourself at the outcome you desire.

You may want to jump back into your life, but the problem is your life has changed. You have changed. And you don't have the energy to start something new again, or even to just keep going.

Because you're tired. Which you have every right to be.

And you may not trust life for the time-being.

So, your job now is to find a way to rest. Truly rest.

Of course there will be competing demands on your attention, and you won't want to rest. Or, you'll feel you can't.

But if you rest in the way that works for you, then this is what will save you.

Because one day you'll rise from your resting period, and you'll realize you're a new, better, stronger you. Lessons learned will no longer feel like mistakes burned into you. You'll be smarter, wiser, kinder, and more humble, yet you'll know you have this fierceness inside that can go to the depths of the darkest night and not tap out. And you'll see, in theory and in practice, that this applies to all areas of your life.

You'll also know better. Which means, when caregiving comes around again, you'll do it differently.

Maybe you'll care the same amount, but of all the people you're caring for, you'll also include you. Caregiving may look different. And that's not only okay. It's good.

What's not okay is if you fall into the same patterns and neglect your needs, your health, your feelings, and your life as you're caring for others.

So, that's your job: to know yourself so truly and deeply that regardless of what comes your way, you'll never betray yourself again.

Spring

Do you remember that visualization list I wrote as a sophomore in college?

1. I am married to Dan.
2. We live in New York City where I practice law.
3. We have one child when I am 34–36 years old.

As I sit here in my home in Manhattan, I can tell you all three of these dreams came true. My husband and I recently celebrated

20 years together! He is still the man of my dreams, even more so as I've watched him proudly and without hesitation step into the role of "Papa" to our soon-to-be three-year old son. It took us awhile to have our son—five years of infertility and IVF—but the resilience needed during the journey came from my lessons learned in compassion fatigue… and awakening from it.

Throughout the day our home is loud and messy. We joke that our son, Hudson, leaves love notes in Cheerios, scattered across our home and his childhood, just like my Dad's notes were spread through mine. I tell Hudson every day that I love him and I'm so proud of him. And I thank him for existing.

Because existing, my dear friends, *your existence*, in the way that is unique to you, is the most important present and act of service you can give the world.

One of my most favorite things is watching my mom and Hudson spend time together. They are best friends, and I love how my mom treats him, with serious consideration and attention to his thoughts, feelings, and questions. As both my mom and our cat, Leo, are aging, Leo has moved into my mom's home, where he revels in the respite from our toddler, and serves as a lap companion and cuddle buddy to my mom.

And in terms of my Dad and Hudson, I like to think that in the five years we were praying for Hudson but before he was Earthside, he was hanging out with Dad. It's not that my Dad never met Hudson; my Dad met Hudson first.

It's like that same time-warp with my three dreams written my sophomore year of college. Sometimes dreams take time—most of the time dreams take time—but for a dream to come true, it has to exist as a thought in your head and a wish in your heart.

God is not asking you to make it happen. He's only asking you to dream it can happen, because that dream opens you up to possibility, and possibility is your ticket to the entire world.

Summer

I know my best days are in front of me, and I know your best days are in front of you.

This isn't because of your past, but because of what I'm certain is included in your future. And what is included in mine.

Just like the rules of compassion fatigue, there is also the rule for dreams, and it's actually quite simple: dreams come true, or something better happens.

As a lawyer and entrepreneur in New York City, I'm a Family Caregiving Attorney and Coach, where I help family caregivers with legal issues, and I help coach family caregivers on self-care, legacy preservation, and dream-building. My pain, my whole Winter's worth of pain, has become my passion and my professional purpose.

Don't discard your dreams now because caregiving makes them feel inconvenient, or selfish, or unattainable. Don't erase your dreams because you're too tired, or too sad, or too old. If you abandon your dreams, you abandon yourself. And you deserve so much better than that.

Please always remember your passport to the Universe is possibility. And it is yours, free of charge. All you need to do is be brave enough to dream.[1]

Tea Light Candles

[1] For resources on compassion fatigue, caregiving, dream-building, and legacy, please visit cozycaregivercafe.com/peace.

Melted Rainbow Ice Cream

Weightless

*When all the burdens
are cut loose
and you rise*

    past the thunderheads

        beyond the crowded cacophony

            into peaceful silence

            *you will find me
waiting to wrap you
like a sun-warmed blanket*

                  *there
we will float together in the void
the only sound our slow breath
the only weight our bodies pressing into each other
our only view the entirety of creation*

Margaret Stauffer, MS, LMFT

Margaret is a licensed marriage and family therapist with over 40 years of experience working with individuals and families around health-related challenges and trauma. A native Californian, she grew up in rural Napa County and has lived throughout the state. Margaret enjoyed a 30 year career with Cancer Support Community as Program Director and Chief Mission Officer. She was a master trainer in Open to Options, a decision support intervention, and participated in the organization at a national level. Having recently retired, Margaret is enjoying daily walks, yoga, golf and the pleasure of no longer being on a schedule. After she renews her LMFT license, she plans to learn Spanish and practice tai chi. She is looking forward to where her next chapter will lead her.

Margaret Stauffer, MS, LMFT

When Professional and Personal Collide

I knew from a young age that I wanted to help people heal from emotional pain. As the youngest child of a family of five, I often observed agonizing arguments between my parents and older brothers (it was the turbulent 1960s and 70s). As a result, I tried to stay under the radar, and I avoided conflict as much as possible. This led me to study psychology in college and then go on to get a master's degree in marriage and family therapy. I wanted to better understand relationships and how to create meaningful connections.

In my early 20s, several things happened close together. When I was 23, my mother was diagnosed with breast cancer. I was already out of the house, focused on being an independent adult, so I was somewhat removed from the trauma she was experiencing. She spoke very little of her experience and the radical mastectomy which left her disfigured. For five years after that, she was cancer free although she had lymphedema that sometimes made it very painful for my musician mother to play the piano.

I worried about getting breast cancer because of her history. It was a huge relief to me when a doctor explained that since she was older when diagnosed, my chances of getting cancer were not greater than those without a family history.

Sadly, my mother began experiencing major back pain. She had a spine x-ray, but the radiologist missed metastases to her spine which were only found by another doctor when she became unable to walk. I was living in San Francisco at the time and didn't have a car, and she was in far northern Napa County, more than an hour's drive away. On the weekends, I'd take the bus to visit her. First in the hospital, and then later at home. I was very scared for her, and this time I really wanted to show up for her. I knew that my father was emotionally unavailable, and I wanted her to have a space to be supported. We talked frequently, and I was able to help care for her. However, she didn't want to burden me and didn't speak much about how it was for her to learn to walk again and go through radiation treatment.

In 1986, my mother was discovered to have metastases to her lungs and started undergoing chemotherapy. While I was living in Southern California, I was able to go to Napa to visit her, and we shared how much we loved each other and had long hugs. She seemed to be doing well with chemo but unexpectedly had a brain aneurysm and died shortly after my visit. So, her cancer had been chronic, and her death was sudden. I missed her terribly and felt orphaned even though my father and brothers were still alive.

Six years later, I was living in San Diego and had just read Gilda Radner's book, "It's Always Something," about her struggle with cancer. She spoke so highly of an organization called The Wellness Community where she received support while she had ovarian cancer. I learned that there was a Wellness Community in San Diego, and I applied to work there as a group facilitator. As soon as I walked in the door, I felt like I belonged. My professional life revolved around TWC from then on. As program director, I was responsible for ensuring that the services we provided were warm, compassionate, and professional. I was often the first point of contact with those who were in distress, newly diagnosed, or reeling from news of a recurrence. At that time, many cancers were often fatal, and I and the other staff often deeply felt the loss of people we had been supporting.

What kept me from experiencing burnout or compassion fatigue was extremely supportive leadership, plus our weekly clinical team meetings. There, we had two hours every week to be with each other, talk about challenges, get feedback, and support each other in the work we were doing every day. This weekly touchpoint kept us grounded and energized to continue leading support groups, meeting with individuals and families, and providing other services to help people affected by cancer live as well as possible. For the 30-plus years that I worked at The Wellness Community, which was later renamed Cancer Support Community, the weekly meetings were critical. My colleagues were my community, my touchpoint.

People often asked me if the work was depressing. I didn't find it so. It felt deeply authentic. Those dealing with cancer are often more open to change and growth than at other points in their lives. It was a privilege to witness someone deciding to change careers to make the most out of their lives. Or gaining the courage to leave bad relationships in search of more connection. Or to incorporate better self-care practices (meditation, exercise, dietary change) and make themselves a priority. I was often so moved by how people found ways to cope and sometimes enrich their lives through the experience.

What I also observed is how challenging it was for the loved ones and carers of those with cancer. They were often more taxed and stressed than those going through treatment. They were always challenged in taking care of themselves while caring for others.

This observation led me to the importance of my own self-care. I didn't want to burn out or become sick from the stress of holding others' pain. I took up yoga and found it to be deeply restorative and meditative as well as a good workout. I made sure that I had time outside each day to walk and take in the beauty of the natural world. Time away to recharge was key as well. Taking several trips each year to beautiful locations helped to reset my stress level. I looked for opportunities to laugh, to find humor and lightness. These practices enriched my life.

However, when faced with more personal caregiving, I felt overwhelmed and challenged. First, my oldest brother suffered a subdural hematoma, and I was responsible for making his health care decisions when he was unable to do so. We had never been close, as he was 10 years older than I. I felt both compassion and frustration when it came to him. My compassion came from knowing that he had borne the brunt of my father's unmet expectations. He had also lost his only son, who was 19 when he suffered a brain aneurism, and my brother had to make the difficult decision to take him off life support. My frustration came from all the bad life choices he made subsequently. One of those choices landed him in prison at San Quentin for several years. I had to move his things out of his apartment and get them stored. I was so angry with him. It was hard to find my compassion at that time.

With this latest health crisis, I was thrust into making decisions for my brother even though we had never discussed his preferences. When he was discharged from the hospital to an acute rehab facility, the phone calls with health care providers and the weekly trips to visit him took me out of my self-care routine. Working daily with those dealing with cancer, along with managing his needs, felt like too much, especially since we had never had a close relationship. I also regularly visited my very elderly father several hours away who had just experienced the loss of his spouse. I knew that my feelings of being overwhelmed sometimes resulted in feeling frustrated or irritated with my brother, my father, my spouse, or the people I supported through work. I especially resented individuals who behaved as though they were entitled. Here I was, caring for everybody, and they expected more.

At Cancer Support Community, everything is provided free of charge, yet this sometimes seemed to increase the sense of entitlement that some members displayed. Complaints always came to me. As with my brother, I vacillated between feeling compassion for what they were dealing with and annoyance. I was grateful that

CSC was a place where they could express their anger or frustration even when it seemed unreasonable to me. At the same time, I would have liked some gratitude back!

I eventually came to terms with the reality that I could only do so much and be there to the extent that I could. I had to practice compassion, not only for my brother and father, but even more for myself. I learned to acknowledge that I was doing the best I could, given the circumstances. I couldn't meet all their needs, just as I couldn't meet all the needs of those I worked with at Cancer Support Community. I really had to continually work at coming from a compassionate place, and often recalled Marshall Rosenberg's characterization of "the tragic expression of unmet needs" that comes across as off-putting or accusatory and ends up alienating the very people they want support from. Only then could I continue to find ways of being there and connecting with difficult people. At least some of the time!

During the most trying times, I also found that certain mantras were helpful to me when I couldn't do anything else. I was at least directing positive energy and intent toward them. "May you be free from suffering. May you be free from fear and anxiety. May you experience peace and joy." Sometimes I would repeat the phrases for quite some time. I could also direct the phrases toward myself.

The last caregiving experience that was of a personal nature was with my father, who at the age of 103 had been living independently. He was found unconscious and was transported to the hospital. At first, he couldn't speak and was very confused. Ultimately, he began to be able to communicate and was moved from the hospital to a skilled nursing facility for rehab. He was there for three months, and I travelled several hours multiple times a week to visit him and engage with his medical team. Ultimately, they had to plan for his discharge, and they suggested a board and care setting for him as he could no longer live on his own and needed too much care for me to have him at my home.

I looked at a number of board and care facilities closer to where I lived, none of which I liked. The facilities cared for people who had much less capacity than my father. Often, they were dark and depressing. I reluctantly settled on a care home recommended by a colleague who had a lot of familiarity with board and care homes. My father was not happy and really missed where he had been living. He kept asking to return there, and I felt horrible telling him that it was no longer an option.

I visited him several times each week for six months until his death. Each time, I had to brace myself to go into the home, interact with the other residents and staff, and spend time with him in his room. Again, it felt like the time spent with him was never enough from his perspective. This took a toll on my time, energy, and outlook. I didn't realize how much of a toll until after his death. I can take comfort that his death was peaceful and without pain. He did have a wonderful care provider at the facility whom he liked. He also died right before the pandemic lockdown, and I'm grateful that he didn't have to go through his last days without me there.

Later, it was helpful to have friends and colleagues to talk to about his death and get support for the multitude of feelings I was experiencing, including relief. I could eventually laugh at how he always had MSNBC on, something that was very annoying to the owner of the board and care facility, who favored FOX.

I realize that in many ways I had it (caregiving) easy. Ninety-nine percent of the time I loved my job supporting people impacted by cancer. I had the capacity to be there for our participants, but the capacity was affected by caregiving close to home. I also realize that for some, caregiving for loved ones isn't days or months, but years. That prolonged and often grueling task interferes with ways of self-care that could support them. Nonetheless, there are some things that can be integrated into our lives to dampen the never-ending demands of caregiving. So I would suggest these ways of supporting oneself and avoiding compassion fatigue:

- Consciously focus on taking time to just breathe deeply for several rounds. This can help to reset your nervous system and can be done anywhere and anytime.
- Practice being kind to yourself. Give yourself credit for what you are doing. Tell yourself supportive things that you would say to a friend going through a similar situation. That kindness and compassion toward yourself will help you be kind to those you are caring for. If you don't care for yourself, it will be hard to care for others.
- Look for ways to connect with others who may be experiencing similar challenges. The camaraderie and sense of community can help you feel understood and supported, and you can learn from others who are dealing with caregiving as well.

- Figure out something you can do for you, whether it is taking a break outside, listening to music, meditating, or watching a movie. This helps to replenish your reserves so you have the capacity to continue doing what you must do.
- Care for yourself physically. Take time to eat, move, and follow your preventive healthcare. If you break down physically, you won't be able to care for others.

I was fortunate to have extremely supportive leadership and experienced professionals to help me learn along the way, and I tried to be that same kind of supportive leader for the many interns and clinicians I trained and managed through my career. Caring for others is a difficult calling whether you choose it as a profession or are thrown into it through family connections, so learning to take care of yourself is as important as finding the energy and time to care for others.

Larry Brouder

For over 28 years, Larry has worked within the Global Employee Mobility industry, creating and managing immigration and benefits, business continuity, and global talent management programs. He has also designed expatriate programs and security and pandemic protocols for the nation's largest privately held engineering firm, and been a consultant on product and business development, business structure, and innovation. He now works for the world's most advanced EV manufacturer. Larry is a regular speaker at HR industry events on topics including Expatriate and Intercultural Programs, Immigration, Global Security, Immigration, and Pandemic Protocol. He lives in Guilford, CT with his family.

Larry Brouder

How to Strengthen Your Compassionate Self

I've always envied the Dalai Lama. I suppose that's some sort of karmic sin in some book somewhere, but to remain compassionate in the environments we tread is a miracle in and of itself, and given what he has been through, it really should be easy for the rest of us.

As I started to think more about compassion, I thought of my younger life in a pretty bad home environment, where the unthinkable was always directed toward my older siblings, who no doubt had it far worse than I did. (My parents maybe thought that their last-born kid was worth shielding from some of the stuff they doled out). I thought about my current role at work, supporting thousands of people in very traumatic situations of relocating or immigrating, not knowing where they may be allowed to live next. Can you imagine that? Wanting to work, being skilled at something, and being asked to apply that skill, but not being allowed to enter a country that needs your skills because of protectionist leanings?

If we really want to solve things like that, don't build a wall. Fund education in STEM like it's the most critical thing to global competition, because it is. But I digress.

Then I thought of my early battle with depression—I won, by the way (I think), mostly because I started to see depression as an asshole trying to take the beauty of life away from my every day. I remember the day of that shift when I was a kid, the morning I won the battle over depression. I remember it vividly, as if I can see the position of the leaves on the trees.

I lay in bed well into the beautiful May morning, speculating on ways that today could possibly be worse than yesterday. It was easy to come up with options: relationships, grades, parents who were so off the rails that we essentially raised ourselves. The choices were endless if I stayed deep enough in my mind. And then, something really started to piss me off.

It was deafening. And musical. And natural. And it woke me out of three years of sleepwalking that is still far too common in teens and tweens across the world. This noise was coming from a finch, and I was trying to sleep away the day. I had to get up and get rid of it somehow. It was messing with my vibe. Screw that finch.

But life had me totally exhausted. I was a pretty small kid, and until then I had been you-must-be-this-tall-to-ride-this-ride obstructed. There was a pecking order in the neighborhood. This construct usually led to a good thrashing by my friend Brian, or some stuffing into lockers at school, and the constant dumping of books as I rushed to classes I would ignore my way through. As my tweenage years mounted, and I stayed small (into mid high school I was about 5' 2", with a twin sister who was at least 5' 4"), I figured I'd never get out. I hated myself for not growing. For not being an athlete like my brother Doug, a brain like my sister Diane, an artist like Lisa, or a musician like my twin sis Linda (fabulous voice, by the way).

Then I found someone to commiserate with, a girl up the street who I had a crush on. She took misery to a whole new level. We could mope away weeks if left to our own designs, and even when spending time together, we could feel utterly alone. Misery truly loves company and invites all sorts of things in the door. So we lived on our common ground, in front of a TV that spit out constant reports on the cold war's progress (or lack thereof) and the initial stirring of divisions in the country that have matured to what we have today.

The months ate away my freshman and sophomore years. My grades were less than mediocre. Winters were too cold, summers too hot, spring too rainy, and fall was when everything died. Had I listened to the Cure and the Smiths at that point, it would have been all over.

It was exhausting. I remember my family making fun of the way I would constantly say "oh, forget it" and resign myself to living without whatever it was I was asking them to forget. The constant effort of searching for the worst and finding it, the validation of the holes in my life, and the self-loathing and abuse were like a daily marathon on a hot beach. Being hard on ourselves is quite a lot of work.

Then, this frigging finch. I only wanted to sleep. Just a few more minutes to burn some daylight so I wouldn't have to figure anything out. But it persisted. I didn't even know what it was at first. My brain was just hell-bent on stopping the noise.

As a kid, and even as a young adult, I had always sabotaged relationships. Get too close, and I'll find a way to push you out. Learn too much, dig too deep. Any relationship was bound to be too taxing, to exposing, too much. When I think of the friends I had lost touch with before that day, it makes my head spin. I figured I was better off with a "simpler" life, and they were better off without me. And here was this persistent little bird, calling me out on the whole thing. With no real stake in the game, nothing to gain in its ceaseless song, it was forging a relationship on the simplest of terms. And I was tired of the fight.

But I arose, intending to shut the bird up. Then: The smell of newly-sprung leaves, in their early-season viper green (my absolute favorite color). The puffy clouds. The deepest blue sky. A gentle, cooling breeze breathing new life into the room, as if its mission was to clear the cobwebs out of my lungs and get me moving in a different direction. And the sunshine. The immediate promise of an empty, beautiful day within which to do something amazing.

It was like being smacked in the head with a fluffy boot filled with puppies and candy and first kisses and songs yet to be written and a world of places to explore and successes of all kinds.

It was the awakening of a kid to the idea of compassion for oneself. Of understanding of the heart of a bully, challenged to find their own place, and why they chose you so frequently (even if the bully was you). Of what the pace of a life should be, how work and consistency and practice lead to the development of something really special that is truly your own. To drop the comparisons we are forced to watch on an endless stream of shows and ads that present someone else's idea of a better you. To take the first step in the journey of a thousand miles, embracing the fear that will motivate the best development of the strongest self.

That's the beauty in it—there are amazing things happening all around you at every minute. It's not that there aren't difficult things and ugliness in the world; there are. But there's stuff the universe is trying to show you that is worth persevering for. The way water freezes at the edge of a stream. A frog stuck to your window. A knowing smile.

And so I got up, looked outside, and chose to walk out the door instead of return to bed.

When we think of compassion, we think of compassion toward others. Of empathy, sympathy, love, etc., etc. Always directed outward. But sometimes it's good to direct that compassion inward. Understand our own point on the planet and be graceful enough to create a clearing for rest and reflection, or a forge to build strength.

That morning with the finch was the shift.

Now, fast-forward 44 years. To today, in fact. Because as I write this, the fantastic company I am blessed to work for is undergoing a reduction in force. Everyone in Silicon Valley seems to be doing it right now—it's quite the fad. This morning started with a three a.m. wake-up, as the dog decided to bark at an unknown, and likely furry, entity on the back porch. That got me up, and I noticed the beckoning glow of a message hitting my phone. A coworker who I was assisting with immigration support (part of what I do now) was let go by the company, in the middle of a trip to his home country, where he was in the process of getting his new work visa.

The employee had recently sent me what seemed to be hundreds of emails on his ongoing immigration process, most starting with headings like "Calamity" and "Complete Chaos" even while things were entirely on track. Now, I'll admit, he wore me down, and he wore me out. The ongoing barrage of affirmations of policy and procedure and place and timing and re-affirmation of those things and changes in schedule and shifting intentions and concerns and then another loop or ten around the same block, over and over again, would tire out Muhammad Ali in his prime.

These inquiries and cycles hit my team on a daily basis in both good and bad times. With over a thousand people on our watch at present, and over 900 people relocating at any given time, the five of us are a trauma center, a triage to get people help and support through a vendor network that is nothing short of a group of angelic and hyper-intelligent superheroes. There are also a lot of cases where we just need to listen, since things are on track but the employee is having a moment of uncertainty.

Some days the immigration inbox we share only gets about 500 emails, and our individual boxes only get about 300. Some days if people don't hear back, they show up in person at our desks. The other day, while I was in a meeting, someone sent an email, then tried to reach me through a call on Slack, then visited my desk, then called my cell phone… all about something routine that they had already been advised on. Each day, we enter the environment fresh and ready to go, with a list of reports and projects and system implementations and action items that grow like evil little dandelions that bite at our heels as we run through the day.

And then there are the impacts of the cultures of the people we support, who come from all over the world. People ask for things differently, answer questions differently, and struggle with language barriers as we guide them through a legal system that is overburdened with minutiae. Some come from places where it is ok to badger until they get what they want. Some come from places where it is impolite to ask for anything. And all won't stop until their place here is secured, their work and family are safe, and they are solidly in the comfort of a normal life with no more forms to fill out until tax time.

They never let up. And I don't blame them. But my team and I do get exhausted. The team has turnover. The company has shifts and turns that are unexpected. But there are days when I want to drive into the hills and keep on going until I get to Canada. Or Mexico. Or Azerbaijan. But I know if I got to the border, someone would be there asking a question. Damn.

Everyone is going through something. Maybe something huge, that will change the direction of their life. Maybe something tiny but challenging, like a leaky pen or the need to get gas on the way to work. These somethings accumulate like stinging snowflakes. Sometimes, most times, on any given day, it just becomes a bit too much. Where we would normally show compassion for the very real plight of someone who may be forced to return to a country that doesn't want them back (or in extreme cases, may literally want them dead), those snowflakes start their stinging, so we start to brush them off without attending to them.

As we brush, they multiply. They smear and cover everything with ice. They cover our glasses, our desk, our computer screen. But the exhaustion beckons us toward inaction and the promise of ignorance-induced bliss. Maybe we should just quit. That would be the easiest way out. Or maybe we can "quiet-quit," doing just enough until someone shows us the door. At least that way we will be getting something out of it all…

And then, once again, the finch arrives.

For me it was a twenty-something guy in the tech group. He was from a world away—ten thousand miles or more. He spoke in a language that was lightning fast and an accent that was hard to understand. He brought me a problem like everyone else. And I was buried in them. But instead of an email, there he was, standing at my desk.

His next immigration step, the start of the process to gain permanent residency, was held up by an approval that was taking a lot of time.

"These things happen—I'll check on it and get back to you," was one of my first options to say.

But as he stood there, talking about what being here would mean to him and his new wife, the sound changed. The grating ping of those stinging snowflakes turned into an odyssey: the story of a young family and the promise of a country I truly love (yet sometimes take for granted). The vow to work for it, harder than anyone, to make sure that the company would get something for their support.

Looking into the eyes of someone in the midst of that plea while they share tales of things you will never experience because you were privileged enough to be born where the opportunity is there for the taking (for some), you stand up. You represent. You feel. And if there's any strength or heart or compassion left, you act.

I felt like the Grinch when his heart grows three sizes, and he picks up the sled (and finally recognizes Max the dog). These were human beings in crisis who were far more similar to me than I had remembered. All they wanted was to have their contribution recognized so that the chance (not the guarantee) of life, liberty, and the pursuit (not automatic distribution) of happiness was on the table.

It's not a handout. It's a deal. It's a fair trade. It's the fuel that has always made America function—new ideas and grit. If I'm anything, I'm fiercely patriotic. That patriotism stems from my own journey. Where I gave myself some grace, walked out the door, and got to work. Where self-compassion allowed for flaws but didn't excuse laziness. Where I could recognize that others were supportive, and take the extended hands where needed, with the promise of giving back at some point.

Now it was time to give back. The global village needed me, and I needed it. My company needed it. The country, contrary to popular belief, needed it. And it started with one person. Now, with understanding based on that one engagement, I'm ready for the next 1,000. The next 10,000. Keep them coming! I'll welcome them and vigilantly support and defend their right to be here, and I'll care about each and every one.

As a kid, I liked the snow. Apart from it being a great source of income (I'm a capitalist to the core and we grew up pretty broke, so I taught myself how to shovel), snowflakes coat the ground with a beautiful, sparkling blanket of white that makes all of us, every house, everything the same. They quiet everything down. They slow the pace of life to enjoying the essentials. They force a real and honest relationship with nature and those around us.

So where are we left after all this?

I've grown to understand that (or have created my own definition around it) compassion is understanding the struggle behind the beauty in others, and doing what you can to help them realize it. While everyone seems to fight over empathy and sympathy and the competition around who cares more, it may be better to go local. There's not much we can impact apart from those around us, and the way we show up for them and respond to them. If, as I found in my teens, we collapse into our own black hole, we start to pull in the beauty around us until it is swallowed up and disappears. Better to look out and engage with what's around us. It may seem impossible at first. But as the old adage goes, the journey of a lifetime begins with a single step. Just be open to the possible. Notice the flower in the sidewalk.

Then it may be about finding that everyone, even the most seemingly successful, have struggles that they have a hard time sharing and solving for. When we hear these while self-focused, we get competitive and defensive, and may immediately gravitate toward what we are facing and diminish the challenges our friends and acquaintances are facing.

It's not that we need to ignore what we face—we need to face what we are challenged with and fight it with all our might. It's an Olympic year, and as I write this, the amazing Simone Biles is back and gearing up for a fierce global competition in gymnastics. She has grit and determination and skill and intelligence and poise, and she defies gravity. But she struggles. And once she opened up about her struggles, she was ready again to compete. At first, many doubted what she was saying based on her prior accomplishments. But once she opened up about it, she also opened the door for other athletes to talk about the impact and anxiety that performing at such a high level may create. So, it's ok to share. And in sharing, we might open a discussion where we find solutions for each other.

Shared experiences are really what makes it all worthwhile. We can go from envy to understanding, and from understanding to care and support. Compassion lives in all of us and shows itself in moments when we may or may not be ready to deploy it. As with the Dalai Lama, we are all the embodiment of compassion. Snowflakes will always light upon your nose. A finch will always sing.

Listen for the finch.

Waiting

Teatime comes late on Thursday.
Construction trucks rumble
Behind the garden fence
Where Linda says the drug dealer used to live
They're building capitalism back there
Digging up the acorns planted by wiser men

Jessica brings the tea and petite shortbread
Like flower petals
Linda grumbles "late again"
And snatches up the shortbread
But I don't mind
Because Jessica has the kindest smile

Buttercups with Cemetery Behind

Cat in Window

Faith Albright, DVM

Faith is the founder of One Living Sanctuary, a haven for rescued farm animals in the San Francisco Bay Area. Having a deep connection with animals all her life, Faith became vegan after visiting her first farm sanctuary at 25 years old, when she dedicated her life to help end animal suffering. Faith began what would be a 20 year journey to begin her own sanctuary by earning a degree in evolution, ecology, and biodiversity from UC Davis, followed by her veterinary degree from the University of Illinois. After working for several years as a shelter vet in San Francisco, Faith realized her dream, and the sanctuary was founded in 2018. She then launched her own business providing home euthanasia services. Outside of work, Faith enjoys culinary arts, meditation, biking, and almost any outdoor activity. She lives with her blind pitbull, Hope, and rescue cats Luna, Nel, Silby, and Edward.

Faith Albright, DVM

Love is Never Wasted

Another animal abuse case was handed to me at the city shelter. Today an emaciated dog—a sweet, tormented Great Dane—looked up at me from eyes impossibly deep, brown, and sunken. Clearing my mind and breathing deeply, I came to him with the most gentle and tender energy I could cultivate. "You're ok, love." I willed him to feel the words as I carefully examined his body and made notes. "We'll protect you. You'll have food and care."

As the veterinarian for the city, I had to do both physical exams on live animals and postmortem examinations on animals who had died of suspected abuse. I learned over time that the stress I carried in my body was in fact secondary trauma. I would often invalidate my own stressed feelings by asking myself, "They went through the pain. Why would I be experiencing stress?"

Investigating each case meant spending hours dwelling on these horrible situations by examining and trying to determine exactly what had happened to the sweet, innocent creature in front of me. I would feel it with them. The starvation, the fear, the pain of injuries or neglect by the very people tasked with caring for them. I thought these abuse cases I was exposed to over the years would be the hardest part of working at the shelter, but the hardest emotional experiences were the daily tasks. They were the little moments that seemed commonplace and were so hard. I would tear up while walking up and down the aisles of animals who had done nothing wrong and did not understand but who were locked up in cages and kennels. They would look at me with pleading eyes, whine as people would pass, begging, "Please help. Please let me out. I'm afraid."

Animal shelters are not the problem. They are an artifact of a society that does not see animal life as sacred and precious, a side effect of careless breeding and impulsive decisions to get a pet without committing to them for life.

As the shelter vet, I also found myself in the role of counselor or almost parent for the people I met. Foster parents would come to me sobbing with a little kitten, three weeks old, who despite their best efforts had faded and died. They couldn't make sense of the death of this tiny baby, the loss of years of life. I would hold the foster parents in a tight hug. I would share with them the logical, spiritual sense I had made of these deaths.

"Who am I to say how long a life should be? Maybe three weeks was the perfect amount of life for this little one. For his entire life, he was loved deeply and kept warm and safe. His person would wake multiple times a night, and throughout the day, to feed him. She held him in her hands and breathed that she loved him. That life sounds pretty sweet, really. And of course it hurts to lose him. You wanted more time to love him. What if grief is not so much overwhelming pain as overwhelming love? The love may feel stuck in you, like it has nowhere to go now that this little one cannot receive it. Your love still matters. That love is not wasted."

The city shelter was an open-door shelter, meaning we could not turn away animals. There is a misnomer in the sheltering industry, calling shelters "kill" or "no kill." The more accurate description is open door (no animals turned away) and closed door (those that get to pick and choose). I was fortunate to work in a shelter with a very high live release rate. Generally speaking, the only animals euthanized were suffering from such severe physical or behavioral issues that rehabilitation was not possible.

This did not make these deaths easier. I would fall in love with every animal I met. An adorable, goofy pup, Eric, made of solid muscle, with an unfortunate taste for chihuahuas. I would see him every day for three weeks while his path was determined. I would play with him in the yard, and watch my colleagues give him toys and treats as he begged for more ear scratches and belly rubs. Options exhausted, the day came when he had to be euthanized. How could one explain to the next devastated chihuahua parent why he was allowed out again? It isn't a punishment. No one there was mad at Eric. We brought him out to the yard and played with him as hard as we could. We brought him the best treats—you want Taco Bell? Yes! Huge candy bar? Yes! He didn't notice the sedative going in and fell asleep very happy, surrounded by people who adored him. I soaked his fur in my tears as he passed. One of my coworkers chided, "You shouldn't love them so hard." I responded stubbornly, "Love is never wasted."

The people who work within these walls are often as traumatized as the animals they care for. People with neurodivergence, trauma, introverted types; those who struggle with fitting in or who don't feel "normal" are often drawn to be around animals. There is an impossibly high rate of domestic violence survivors among the workers. While working at the shelter, I was seen by my colleagues and friends, and they gently held space for me to examine my own situation. At the time, I was in an abusive relationship. When I finally went to a woman's shelter for help, they handed me a brochure that asked what type of abuse I was experiencing: physical, sexual, emotional, psychological, financial, spiritual, or technological. My answer was yes. All of them.

My rock-bottom was denying the stress, the difficulty, the spinning out of control in both my professional and personal life. I kept telling myself that if I just worked harder, if I could just show up better, do more, be better, then I could handle all of it. Around the same time this relationship began and I started working at the animal shelter, I also started meditating and practicing with Buddhist teachers. Through Buddhist teachings and meditating a little bit every day, I was cultivating a feeling of being "ok" even when life circumstances were impossibly hard. One day, after one of the countless counseling sessions with my abusive partner, I stayed behind to ask the counselor what more I could do to fix this.

"Faith," he said, his voice painfully tender. "I'm looking at an exhausted woman. You cannot do more. You cannot have enough emotional maturity or love to compensate for a partner who refuses to try, or change, or grow. You cannot find what you're searching for here."

The volunteers and workers at the shelter would sometimes ask why people did horrible things to animals. Despairing, they would imagine the horrible things they might do to those same abusers if they met them. I would answer gently, "Hurt people hurt people. Or animals in this case. They lash out in a world that seems terrifying because they have already been injured horribly. They need love to heal, not more violence."

Every time I took the train home after a typically draining day at the shelter, I had no idea what mood my partner would be in. A sour mood would mean screaming or even hitting and kicking… I loved him deeply and saw his tortured injured child just under the surface. My partner needed love to heal, and I believed I should love him. My ride was 30 minutes, exactly long enough to take in a guided meditation on healing trauma. I pushed play, took a deep breath, and closed my eyes. On most of these rides—the one peaceful, safe place in my day—I would cry hard and openly. Hot tears burned my face as I listened to the soft words, which brought hope and grounding. Years ago, I had talked myself out of being ashamed of sadness. I never apologize for being happy; why would I need to feel bad about sadness? On one particular commute, I opened my eyes and noticed a man in a business suit on his way home noticing me. His face was filled with such deep compassion and tenderness. I smiled softly at him as if to say, "I'm ok. Thank you for caring." I tried to transmit the thought with my energy.

My public crying did not seem to create a burden for others but instead offered them a doorway into their own deep capacity for compassion and connection. Our hearts all break the same way.

That counselor was right: I *was* exhausted. I learned that year what it meant for me to spiritually bypass my humanness. I felt ok. I knew everything was and would be ok. Even when my days were brutal, I could fall back on presence. Most moments were sweet at best, and neutral at worst, with only a few moments during the day being actually horrible. If I could practice mindfulness, I could endure the difficulty. But I was misusing Buddhist teachings to keep myself trapped in unhealthy environments at work and home. I treated pain and abuse as my pathway to enlightenment and nonaggression. After speaking with therapists, my spiritual teachers, and countless amazing friends and strangers who had been where I was, I started to see my situation more clearly.

My Buddhist teacher gently offered perspective: "You can have love and compassion for everyone, but some people are too dangerous for you to love up close. By staying in this abusive cycle, you are not just allowing harm to come to you, you are participating in keeping the conditions in place that harm both of you. Every time he hurts you, he is also hurting himself." I thought of how my partner would cry every time he hit me, and how often I would comfort him in his confusion and pain and his feeling out of control. My teacher was careful to explain that he was in no way blaming me for the situation and that I had the power to break this harmful cycle.

With clearer vision, I started to understand that my relationship and the job at the shelter were not the best fit for me to create the most positive change in the world. The relationship was exhausting me, and the job was causing trauma in my body faster than I could heal it. On top of it all, upper management was incompetent at best and abusive at worst in how they handled the work environment. Over the next two years, I disentangled from both situations.

Years before, when I was in my early 20s and trying to figure out what to do with my life, I knew that I wanted to find a way to give the most back to the world as possible for one life. I was fortunate to have married my best friend, and we played with ideas over a few years trying to determine the best path forward. My husband was an incredibly kind and wise man who loved animals and wanted to help the world as much as I did. I ran through the career choices I had often thought of before: veterinarian, doctor, chiropractor, midwife… anything to help others. None of them seemed like enough. I wanted to do more. We thought of opening a cat sanctuary, seeing the numbers of them that were euthanized in the shelters where we volunteered. Then, when I was 23, we toured a farm animal sanctuary. I mostly wanted to go to pet the cows. I'd never been able to convince field cows to share a hug with me. During the tour, we learned that of all human-caused animal deaths in a year, just 3% happened in shelters, in labs, at fur farms, or through hunting. The remaining 97%, or 14 billion land animals per year in the US alone, were killed in the animal agriculture industry. That night my husband and I went vegan. Still, it wasn't enough. We decided we would open a farm animal sanctuary. If we could change one heart a year through the opportunity to get to know these sweet beings as more than just packaged meat, that one person would amount to 100 fewer animals killed per year.

Going to vet school and paying off the loans was the first part of this 20-year plan. The plan sounded hard at the outset, but the most challenging parts wouldn't be apparent until far later, when I was working at the shelter. During this low point, my rock bottom, I was going through divorce from my sweet husband at the same time as I was trying to break up with the abusive partner, all while giving more energy than I had to a job that was slowly killing me.

The divorce finalized, and I managed to get out of the abusive relationship with the help of another person who found me, who loved me, and who showed me an alternative. I was determined not to allow the abuse to ever harden me. I will not stop trusting people. I will not stop loving. I finally stopped speaking to my abuser, and later started a new relationship with this new person who had gently offered me a hand when I really needed one.

A few years into our relationship, I announced that it was time for me to start the sanctuary. I figured this might end the relationship, as this lovely human was from central London and saw themself always living in cities, not owning a car, traveling by bike and train. I wanted to move to a place where I could own acres and rescue farm animals. To my great surprise, they agreed to go look at my dream property with me. In February 2019, we toured the farm I had been real estate stalking for five years. It was love at first sight. They agreed to cosign on the mortgage, which I could not qualify for myself, and so our farm, One Living Sanctuary, was born.

I promised myself that mine would not be one of those sanctuaries that became inundated with animals instantly. I was going to be slow to rescue, so that I could keep the rest of my life balanced, as I continued to learn how to practice self-care. I was still working at the shelter to pay the mortgage, and now had three hours of commuting by bike and train to get to and from work every day. Our first animal rescues came from the shelter. An old lady pit bull arrived in my office one day—another abuse investigation. She had been found abandoned in an apartment with no food or water for at least a week. She was blind, her eyes painful with glaucoma and uveitis, emaciated, and impossibly sweet. She just wanted to sit near people and get pets. I spayed her, took out her nonfunctional and painful eyes, named her Hope, and brought her home. Hope became the first sanctuary resident.

I wanted to bring home every animal at the shelter. There is a common story shared in rescue communities about a father and child walking on the beach. The child sees a starfish washed up on the shore and throws it back into the water. Then tosses another back in a few steps further on, and another. The father sees the thousands of starfish stranded on the shore and says, "You can't save them all. It won't make a difference." The child picks up another starfish and says, "I can make a difference for this one." And throws it back. I could not save all the animals I met, but I could save this one.

Hope was quickly followed by three adorable bantam hens: Farrah, Penny, and Sofia. Penny turned out to be a rooster, and so became Pendragon. Days turned into weeks, which turned into months, and our numbers grew to over 50 animal residents. Daily

I would get calls asking to rescue a pig, or a rooster, or a group of goats. We seemed to have space, and with one animal care person, and the two of us working to support the sanctuary, it was easy in the beginning to want to say yes to everyone. We had the space, right?

Learning to say "no" was the first major lesson that needed to happen for me at the sanctuary. The joy of rescue was being muted by the sheer exhaustion of trying to keep up with a more than full time shelter job and commute, then coming home to the 50-plus beings that needed attention at the sanctuary. Having the physical space did not equate to having the emotional, financial, and temporal space for one more rescue. When I would receive yet another heart-wrenching call about an animal that was in dire condition and just needed a place to go, I would breathe and center and remind myself that while I could not save them all, I could make a difference in many lives. I had a responsibility to the lives I had already committed to. I needed to keep all of us healthy and fed. Our numbers stabilized around 100, and since then I've learned how to gently and firmly say, "no."

From my exhausted, nearly burned-out state, I kept reading spiritual books (particularly Pema Chödrön), self-help books, books on healing from trauma, books on communication and healthy relationships. I learned from speaking with people about what has worked for them. I learned to recognize when I was leaning too heavily on spirituality and ignoring some psychological issue that needed attention. I committed to taking better care of myself, eating healthy meals, staying well hydrated, sleeping enough, and exercising. I took to heart the Buddhist idea of "practice." There is no destination—a difficult concept for a recovering perfectionist to believe. It is just a journey, and every day I can learn and do a little better or accept myself with compassion and tenderness. Mindfulness allowed me to assess my body and mind on hard days to know what I was likely lacking. I know that on days when I need a run the most, the inertia is the most difficult to overcome, and that within seven minutes I'll feel an enormous weight lifted off myself. I wish I had known more about the intrinsic relationship of trauma and caretakers. I wish I had known sooner about finding balance, or believed people when they talked about self-care being fundamentally important. I'm grateful to be working toward more balance in my life, and I feel the difference in my work.

As well as working at the animal shelter and getting One Living Sanctuary up and running, I started working on my own home visit veterinary practice. After running the numbers, I saw that I could leave the shelter job and enjoy more flexibility and likely the same pay by moving fully into my own practice. Of all the appointments I did, the most consistently positive feedback I would get was my euthanasia appointments. Even during veterinary school, my fellow students noticed my aptitude for being with people in difficult emotions. They would "helpfully" pass off their cases where people were falling apart to me. With an emotionally intelligent and wise therapist mother, a lifetime of practice with emotionally immature people, and being fascinated with self-help since age 13, I was able to sit easily with challenging emotions. As I would hold space for people to grieve their passing little ones, clients would tell me again and again how much easier I made the process for them. In the autumn of 2019, I finally quit working at the shelter and moved full time into running my own home euthanasia business and growing the sanctuary.

On a typical day, I will have as many as seven euthanasia appointments, mostly cats and dogs. Everyone I speak to is in grief. When people call to make the appointment, their voices often catch, and they apologize. My heart opens to them, and I gently tell them, "It's totally natural to cry. I think our emotions are tied right to our voice. The moment we start speaking, they come out."

I've heard grief described as overwhelming love. That is exactly what I witness during appointments. People answer the door in a daze. Their eyes are red-rimmed, or they are actively crying. They give me a polite, and heartbreaking, smile. I walk them through the process and greet my patient. The animals generally look exhausted, like adored animals at the end of a very happy life, and they are ready to move on. The people are ripped open in grief. There is a beauty to this pain. With the heart open, there is nothing between us. There is no fake, polite chatter. There is only the most pure, raw form of existence.

The scenes at the end are incredibly beautiful and poignant. A man holds his dog's paw and tells his dearest friend, "I will always love you, buddy. I promise I'll never forget." A woman holds her cat in her lap and sobs as she thinks of everything they have shared. Her husband holds her shoulders and kisses her head so tenderly, trying to take on some of her pain. A child lying on her golden retriever and crying into her fur tells her mom, "I have a stomachache in my heart." A couple sitting on an outdoor bench under exquisite flowering fuchsia and jasmine curl their heads together over their fluffy Parisian cat, and a hummingbird hovers around them seemingly tuning into the timeless moment.

Love flows freely. Couples look at each other, deep into exposed souls, and whisper, "I love you so much" over the heads of their dying babies. Children are held tightly. Siblings and friends hug, rub backs, kiss. If people could all see this side of each other, would our hearts open? During a contentious election cycle when it feels the whole country is against each other, I would go from a Trump house to a Hillary home, and everyone would cry the same. A broken heart is the same for everyone.

I guide the humans gently through their emotions and the process. I help the animal transition as peacefully as possible. When their emotions are very intense and I find myself triggered into overwhelm or a flashback of trauma, I pull myself back into my body, notice where my legs and butt are supported by the floor. I take a few deep breaths to ground myself, remind myself that the emotions are theirs, and send out love and peace with each breath. I promise the people they are doing the right thing, that they picked the right moment.

Our society hides death. It isn't really discussed. It certainly isn't celebrated as a natural conclusion to a beautiful life. People often feel guilty, like they are killing this little being they have promised to protect. "I understand why you would feel that way. It's surreal," I reassure, "and you are not ending their life. You are ending their suffering. Life ends. Relationships end. The other side of love is grief. It is always worth it. You didn't fail them." I wrap their friend carefully in a blanket and carry them out like a baby.

I allow myself to fall in love during every appointment. I love the people in their tenderness, in their vulnerability, in this emotion I know so well. I love the animals, their life well lived, the love they gave, the love they received. People think this job must be impossibly hard for me. It is incredibly heart-opening. I love people more every day, and from that place of love and compassion, the work becomes easier. Life becomes easier. There are hard moments, sometimes moments that bring us to our knees, and we feel under an ocean of sadness. Even in those moments, if I can drop the story and just feel the emotions, I can feel the beauty of being alive. If I'm witnessing the pain of others, or going through another breakup, another death, another goodbye myself, when I can allow my heart to soften and open rather than getting hard, or trying to clench around the pain, I find my soul filling up with the sacred love of this life.

No, this is not a hard job for me. This is a beautiful job, and life, and I love it more every day.

Ginkgo Leaves After a Rain

Jean C. Accius, Ph.D.

Dr. Jean Accius is a visionary leader in health equity and systems transformation. As President & CEO of CHC: Creating Healthier Communities, he drives efforts to dismantle barriers to health, empowering communities to thrive. With a deep understanding of cross-sector collaboration, Dr. Accius has developed innovative policies and programs that reveal the economic benefits of addressing disparities. Previously, he served in leadership roles at AARP and the Centers for Medicare & Medicaid Services. His work has earned recognition from Next Avenue, Black Enterprise, and Fast Company, among others. A sought-after speaker and author, Dr. Accius has contributed to discussions at the World Economic Forum and the United Nations. He holds degrees from Florida State University and a Ph.D. from American University.

Jean C. Accius, Ph.D.

Rising Above: A Journey of Loss, Resilience, and the Fight for Equity and Justice

> "I am an invisible man. No, I am not a spook like those who haunted Edgar Allan Poe; nor am I one of your Hollywood-movie ectoplasms. I am a man of substance, of flesh and bone, fiber and liquids—and I might even be said to possess a mind. I am invisible, understand, simply because people refuse to see me."

A Bright New Dawn Awaits

These are the words of Ralph Ellison in his piece "Invisible Man." Ellison shows—and we all know—that human beings, at our deepest core, want to be seen. We want our experiences validated, and we want to know that our voices matter. But what happens when you are invisible? What happens when individuals, organizations, or even professions don't see you… or can't hear you?

I am on a mission to disrupt the systems, policies, and structures in our society that determine who is worthy of certain rights and benefits, leaving others in a state of invisibility with very little access to resources, opportunity, and the ability to live a longer, healthier, and more productive life. This is my "why," which has guided me throughout my personal and professional journey. I know what it's like be invisible in our society—where your environment suggests that you might not matter. Where individuals, health care professionals, and those with authority see *through* you instead of seeing *you*. I know what it feels like to be told you are less than, not good enough, or to be categorized based on the country of your birth. However, I also know the beauty that comes with not being defined by what one lacks and the resiliency that only grows from losses, hardships, and tribulations.

None of us achieves success on our own, and for me, the images that are still clear despite the decades that have passed are of my grandmother, waking up well before the sun rose in Haiti, lifting up her basket of goods and placing it over her head, then heading off to the marketplace. In the evenings, I'd see her return, exhausted after a long day but content knowing she was successful in providing her family with food. My grandmother raised me in Haiti for the first four years of my life.

Around the time of my birth, my mother came to the hard realization that she was not in a position to fully care for me. While this decision pained me for a large portion of my life, I have come to the realization that she made the hard, life-changing decision to place me under my grandmother's care so I could have a better future with opportunities she could only dream of. My grandmother took on this responsibility and sacrificed so I did not go without. With little income and no formal education herself, she made sure I received a high-quality education.

Despite the loss of those years with my mother, I am forever grateful to my grandmother for the decision she made to raise me during those formative years, and for the sacrifices she made in order for me to become the person I am today. Every milestone I've reached in my life, from grade-school graduations, completing my doctoral program, working for the Obama Administration, briefing members of Congress, to becoming President & CEO of a nationwide nonprofit organization, has been something of a thank you to my grandmother.

In a world where it seems everything is changing all the time beyond our control, there is one thing we can count on: every morning, the sun rises, gradually shining its light on the faces of those eager for the promise of a brand-new day. Each ray feels like a beacon of hope for opportunity, second chances, prosperity, renewal, and connection. We busy ourselves with our tasks and to-dos, big goals and big dreams in mind.

In the evening, the sun sets, and we go to bed hoping we're leaving the world a better place for the next generation. We center ourselves at home, wondering why there aren't enough waking hours. We get quiet—really quiet—hoping we've made good choices, and we send out a bedtime wish for peace for all.

Given what we've all lived through these past few years, every sunrise and sunset is a gift. I hesitate to throw out phrases like "post-

COVID this" or "new normal that" because what has happened to humanity is far greater than words can describe. There is no doubt this pandemic turned our world upside down. Loss of life and loss of the everyday things we took for granted will leave lasting, traumatic scars no matter how resilient we are.

The health, economic, emotional, and spiritual toll has been debilitating. Combined with how these issues have affected communities differently, we were forced as a nation to confront our brokenness. That brokenness had always been there, but we were in denial, blind, or indifferent. However, we can no longer as a collective afford to be on the sidelines as the barriers to opportunity continue to grow and become out of reach for those who have been historically marginalized and invisible in our society.

We must create solutions that meet people where they are and ensure there are opportunities for every level of means and aspiration. Right now, this work is more urgent than ever.

Weathering the Storms: The Beauty and Complexity of Life

In *A Tale of Two Cities*, Charles Dickens famously wrote about the best of times and the worst of times. No question, the last few years have been the worst of times. Within days and weeks of the pandemic shutdown in March 2020, millions of people—some of them our friends and family, if not us—lost their livelihoods. Millions around the world died from COVID. Here in the United States, hundreds of thousands of businesses closed, never to re-open. The way we educated our children changed. Communities were fractured and then put back together.

And, with emerging virus variants and ever-changing safety guidelines, anxiety and depression were at all-time highs. Exhaustion ran rampant in households as everyone tried to figure out what a new normal would be for them and their family.

As if millions dying and our way of living turned upside down weren't enough, the United States publicly went through a racial reckoning unlike any other in 2020 that continues today. The first one of its kind, it made people actively explore their contributions and inaction that have led to persistent and systemic racial injustice in America.

Many of us are grieving, whether it's because of the loss of a loved one that shook the very foundation of our being, or the aching pain, bittersweet nostalgia, and longing for what used to be. In reflecting on my own personal journey, 2020 was just a tough year where my personal and professional worlds collided.

In January, I lost one of my grandmothers who was a beacon of wisdom and resolve. Tragically, the losses continued to mount. In early March, my cousin, a young woman full of life with big dreams and aspirations drowned and was found dead in a lake. That same month, my bonus mom was diagnosed with metastatic breast cancer, and the doctors told her that she only had a few months of life remaining. In August, with lockdown in full effect, we were not allowed to be with her as she took her final breaths. Thanks to some amazing nurses and Facetime, I was able to see her face—and she, mine—for one last time. She struggled to get out a few words and sounds when she saw me, and I told her how much I loved her over, and over, and over again as machines beeped in the background and her chest raised and lowered with the assistance of a ventilator. She died the next day, on her 54th birthday.

All of this happened while I was leading and managing a team who had their own personal and professional challenges.

My career and life's work have always focused on increasing access to health care, ensuring those without voices are heard, and creating solutions that meet people where they are. On closing the gaps that exist in our society and ensuring there are opportunities for every level of means and aspirations. On removing barriers that rob people of the chance to live longer, healthier, more productive lives.

I was good at compartmentalizing, but by November of 2020, I found myself exhausted—physically, mentally, and emotionally—and suffering from vertigo for the first time.

We certainly had been through a great deal, yet in some sense, the tough part had only begun. And sometimes, the tough part involves an honest look in the mirror, which makes it possible for our tribulations to not be in vain. The COVID-19 pandemic, the racial unrest, and the loss of life shed a very bright light on the weakness of our systems that were designed to provide the basic foundations that would nurture and secure healthy lives, both at home and around the world. The pandemic, for better or for worse (or both), had drastically changed our societies, our communities, and—in many ways—us.

Time is Everything:
The Fight for Equity and Justice for All

Time is our only non-renewable resource. We can find ways to innovate and produce every other resource on the planet, but once time is spent, there's no getting it back. It's a finite resource with no substitutes or alternates. That makes time incredibly valuable. And expensive.

Time is expensive because time lost has an enormous impact on our well-being, our families, our communities, and our economy. When I talk about time lost, I'm not talking about time we spend annoyed that the school drop-off line is moving too slowly, or time spent in a doctor's office waiting room. I'm talking about time lost due to economic, social, and racial disparities that exist in America. Maybe it's better to describe it as time robbed, more than time lost.

Undergirding COVID has always been the ongoing, decades-long crisis of longevity being determined by where you live, not your genetic code. In Atlanta, for example, life expectancy drops 13 years between Buckhead and Bankhead… two neighborhoods about nine miles apart from each other. If you live in one of those neighborhoods, you don't get to live out the 13 more years that someone in the other neighborhood does. Thirteen years less of life. Think about what you did in the past 13 years. Now, imagine if you hadn't lived to do those things. Does that seem fair to you?

I could share hundreds more examples—the upper east side of Manhattan vs. Harlem… neighborhoods a mile apart in Baltimore… neighborhoods just four Metro stops apart in Washington, DC… and on and on.

Every resident of every neighborhood deserves the same number of years to grow old with their spouses, play cards with their friends, check books out of the library, and watch their grandchildren grow up. People shouldn't be living shorter lives than their counterparts just a few blocks away. It's the antithesis of American values to learn that it's not your genetic code that determines how long you'll live. It's your ZIP code.

And no one should be experiencing hunger or homeless, living in poor health, or suffering a speedier death as an older American. We all have a role and responsibility to advance equity and ensure that everyone has the opportunity to live a longer, healthier, and more productive life.

Closing the disparity gap ensures that people have equal time to love and be loved. If we did that, just think about the possibilities, the opportunities, the equality, the healing, the power, and the prosperity that would fuel our economic, educational, physical, and emotional engines. It would endow us all with the most precious asset of all: time alive on this earth in service to making the world a better place to live and love.

Roadmap:
Translating Pain into Purpose and Action

The tumultuous waves of the pandemic, racial unrest, and the loss of loved ones rocked my world to its core, leaving me adrift in a sea of uncertainty and grief. Yet, amidst the storm, I found solace in the delicate balance of grief, self-compassion, and resilience, summoning the courage to implement strategies for self-care and illuminating a path forward through the darkness.

Be Present

Time is a gift. It is the most expensive currency and one you can never get back once you've spent it. The biggest mistake many of us make is thinking that time is infinite when in fact it is finite. When I think about the last couple of years, I would have given anything to have one last conversation with my mother, grandmother, and cousin.

The idea of being present and thinking about where and with whom I spend my time isn't only about wishing I'd had more time with those who are now gone. It's bigger than that. It's also about my own life and how I want to spend the unknown number of hours I will have on this planet, and dedicating my life to eliminating disparities to ensure that everyone in America has equal access to opportunity.

Hustle Culture is Over

For far too long, success was measured by who can be the busiest and who can grind the hardest. Sacrifice was the mantra. However, I have learned to ask the questions "to what end?" and "at what cost?"

Burnout is real, and it has a ripple effect. There were more moments than I could count over the last four years where I was tired to the bone—you know that feeling where everything hurts or aches, you're running on fumes, and you feel like you're floating above yourself and not really processing information because you have 20 other things to get to next. It's not healthy, and it's surely not sustainable. No one wins—not your family, not your team, and especially not you—when you hit that wall.

Hustle and grind can be a hard habit to break, especially when you're in a profession where your work helps shape how others live and thrive. Still, it's a habit I am resolving to break because these last four years taught me that I must.

Somewhere on the journey into adulthood, we've been conditioned to think that play and joy are just for kids. It's time to reframe that narrative. I am looking forward to setting some new, more healthy boundaries so that I can feed my physical, emotional, and creative soul. Playing, jamming out to music, dancing around the house with the kids or by myself (whether or not anyone else is home), practicing meditation and mindfulness to be more present, traveling to new places or exploring the landmarks in my own backyard, getting the right amount of sleep for me, exploring new hobbies I've always been interested in… these are the kinds of things I need more of in my life, and I bet you might, too.

Self-Care is More Than a Buzzword

It seems like time is moving faster than ever before. It's been difficult to even catch our breath given the pace and speed of how much has changed. However, take a breath we must. It is important to take stock of our mental, emotional, and spiritual well-being. It's doing things that bring you joy. Play more. Laugh more. Watch mindless TV. Crank up the music and the volume while you're at it. Dance. Rest. Sleep. Travel and explore the world around you.

Focus on the constant pursuit of happiness even in the darkest moments. It's mustering the courage to know at your core that you will be okay and that it's okay not to be okay. It's finding peace and stillness in the chaos. It's intentionally looking for things to be grateful about. It's putting on your own mask first—making sure you're not running on empty so you have enough energy to fuel others.

Set a New Pace

Slowing down should not be seen as a negative, just like moving fast should not be seen to be "reckless" or failing to consider all the factors needed to make strategic decisions. It's understanding why pacing matters so much to us—it's the act of identifying what kind of movement is needed and when/how it is needed, to make progress on something. It's neither slow nor fast. It just is. And we need to be thoughtful, purposeful, and adaptable in our pacing.

As I sit here at my desk and think about organizational, professional, and personal priorities, I also am reconsidering their pacing as well as how I can adjust as the year progresses. Just like a long-distance runner factors in hydration, exhaustion, leg cramps, breathing, and terrain—and how those factors might change at a moment's notice—I am being mindful about what considerations go into my own pacing this year. I also want to pay special attention to how those on my team are thinking about pacing their work so we can ensure the best possible outcomes for the projects we invest in.

Leadership: At the Heart of the Common Good Lies Collaboration

The challenges we face are complex and multifaceted, and no single entity can solve them in isolation. By working together with other organizations, governments, and stakeholders, we leverage our collective strength to effect positive change. In our pursuit of a new leadership paradigm, we must confront the dangerous power of fear—a power often used against us. Fear breeds distrust, divides us, and blinds us to the opportunities that lie before us. It is fear that propels the zero-sum mentality, convincing us that someone else's gain must be our loss.

We must break free from this cycle and embrace a future defined by hope and possibility. Our decisions should not be guided by fear but by courage and conviction: the courage to make bold choices that align with our values, even in the face of uncertainty.

Let us rise above the politics of fear and embrace empathy and understanding. Let us actively listen to differing perspectives, recognizing that diverse voices enrich our understanding and open new pathways to success.

I have long been inspired by the late congressman John Lewis. In his book *Across That Bridge: A Vision of Change and the Future of America*, Lewis wrote, "It is only through examining history that you become aware of where you stand within the continuum of change."

If we're lucky, we'll each get 30,000 sunrises and 30,000 sunsets in our life. Let us all commit to honoring where we are right at this very moment in our continuum of change. There is unprecedented opportunity before each and every one of us with every sunrise, and 30,000 chances to lay our head on our pillow at night knowing we have done all the right and good things to leave the world a better place for those who come next.

Cherry Blossoms on a Clear Day

Sally Spencer-Thomas, Psy.D.

Dr. Sally Spencer-Thomas is a clinical psychologist and renowned mental health advocate, driven by personal experience after losing her brother to suicide. Her mission is to amplify the voices of those who have faced mental health challenges, including addiction and trauma, empowering individuals in despair to rediscover their passion for life. Sally focuses on equipping leaders and communities with innovative, sustainable strategies for mental health promotion, addiction recovery, and suicide prevention. She is the lead author of the National Guidelines for Workplace Suicide Prevention and has played significant roles in multiple influential organizations. Sally has delivered a TEDx talk and addressed audiences at the White House. Her global impact spans numerous countries, collaborating with major organizations and initiatives like "Man Therapy" and the Guts, Grit & the Grind book series, aimed at supporting men in navigating life's challenges. www.SallySpencerThomas.com

Sally Spencer-Thomas, Psy.D.

Supporting a Loved One With Mental Health Challenges

My Before and After Moment

Just as people recall exactly where they were during pivotal historical events, the tragic moment that upends a life can etch itself into memory with the same immutable force. For me, December 7, 2004, was such a moment. My life before and after that was very different.

My world irrevocably changed on December 7, 2004, while driving with my three young sons to a holiday celebration with my students to commemorate the end of another semester. I had been on maternity leave that semester and was eager to reunite with them.

My brother Carson, whom I'd been trying to support through his severe bipolar condition, had reached an impasse in his battle. Amidst the regular holiday cheer, a dread churned deep within me, a consequence of months of reacting to his escalating mood volatility.

It had been a challenging fall, and emotional exhaustion had seeped into my bones. After months of being estranged from most of his inner circle friends and family, Carson had come back to us. His reckless, mean, and agitated mania gave way to the worst episode of depression we had ever seen. His mental health condition demanded an ever-present vigilance. The toll on me was a significant emotional drain—compassion fatigue that no one saw, including myself.

That day, on the way to the holiday celebration, a festive air filled my car. I'd glance at the rearview mirror and see my kids snuggled in their car seats behind me. With the fragility of my brother's state and the delicate balance I strove to maintain, it was as if I was always awaiting the next upheaval. Yet, the festive spirit of my students and the anticipation of reconnecting after a long absence gave me a momentary lift.

As we sped down the highway to the party about an hour away, my Nicholas was teaching his three-year-old brother the dreidel song. My car was filled with the scent of cloves from the ham I was bringing to the potluck. I had the Secret Santa gift on the front seat for the gift exchange. After months of distress worrying about my brother, in that moment life was good.

Then the phone rang; the fragile sense of joy and gratitude shattered.

My mother's voice was eerily calm, but my sense of dread quickly escalated. Nothing could have prepared me for the stark reality she relayed.

"Our worst fears have been confirmed. Your brother has killed himself."

The crushing confirmation of my brother's suicide broke me. I screamed. The sound was alien, a manifestation of the pent-up fears, the stifled cries, the swallowed resentments. It was a scream not just of loss but of a profound exhaustion of the soul.

The screams faded into silence, and it was the tender voice of my son, Nicholas, that drew me back into the car.

"Momma... I'm crying for you," he said. Like a laser through the chaos of the moment to my heart.

He knew his uncle as a figure of fun and adventure, not the man tormented by internal chaos that I had come to know in the months leading up to his death. Uncle Carson was a magical figure in Nick's life—teaching him the finer points of shooting pool and how to aim his little skis down the bunny hill.

Six months prior, the onset of Carson's severe bipolar episode triggered a relentless cycle of support and rejection, and I oscillated between hope and despair. His drastic life changes, the emotional turbulence of our relationship, and the constant strain of worry had eroded my resilience, leaving me navigating the fine line between empathy and emotional depletion. Some days I saw the loving, funny brother that I knew well. Other days he was mean and spiteful, and his attacks cut deep. Other days, I only saw his thousand-mile stare.

As support people for loved ones experiencing mental health emergencies, I like many others often don't recognize our descent into compassion fatigue until a crisis jolts us into awareness. We are the guardians of our loved ones' well-being, yet in the process, we risk losing pieces of ourselves.

Before Carson died by suicide, I had been in the field of mental health for about 16 years. After he died, I left the work of therapy completely.

Risks and Rewards of Mental Health Caregiving

Nowadays, mental health care is increasingly happening at home instead of hospitals, which means families have to handle more of the recovery process. Families need to learn how to deal with difficult behaviors like aggression and make sure everyone understands the plan for getting better, including professional support and maybe some financial help.

Lots of research shows that more people are having mental health problems these days. About one in four people in the US will have a significant mental health challenge each year. Most people with mental health issues don't stay in hospitals; they get treated while living their regular lives. But getting better doesn't mean they're in the clear. Many folks might find their symptoms returning—about a third to half within six months, and even more within five years. Thus, mental health caregiving is a role provided in many homes, often without guidance or acknowledgment.

Caring for someone with mental health challenges, despite its demands, can enhance the caregiver's own emotional and psychological well-being. Many caregivers find that their experiences lead to significant personal growth. They often develop greater patience, empathy, and understanding. Facing and overcoming daily challenges can also enhance their resilience, making them stronger in dealing with their own life's adversities.

Providing care can also lead to a deeper connection with the care recipient. Through shared struggles and successes, bonds can strengthen, which can be deeply rewarding. This closer bond is often cited as one of the most meaningful aspects of caregiving. Many caregivers feel a profound sense of purpose and fulfillment from being able to help a loved one in a very tangible way, and they feel a sense of accomplishment and pride in managing both the small and significant challenges that come with caregiving. There's often love, joy, and gratitude amid the stress of caregiving.

Caring for individuals with mental health issues can bring on a trio of related stresses:

- **Compassion Fatigue**

  This is often experienced by those who provide care to others in distress. It arises from the emotional residue or strain of exposure to working with those suffering from the consequences of traumatic events. It differs from burnout but can co-exist. Compassion fatigue can occur due to exposure to just one intense support relationship, or it can be cumulative over many.

- **Burnout**

  This is a state of emotional, physical, and mental exhaustion caused by excessive and prolonged stress. Burnout is characterized by emotional exhaustion, depersonalization, and reduced personal accomplishment. Caregivers feel overwhelmed and unable to meet constant demands. If it goes on too long, mental health caregivers can start to detach from their work and their lives. As the stress continues, they begin to lose the interest and motivation that led them to take on a certain role in the first place.

- **Secondary Traumatic Stress (STS)**
Sometimes called "vicarious traumatization" or "secondary trauma," this is the emotional duress that results when an individual hears about the firsthand trauma experiences of another. Secondary Traumatic Stress is a significant concern for mental health caregivers who are regularly exposed to the traumatic experiences of others, as they are often privy to the intense, distressing narratives and behaviors associated with these conditions. Mental health caregivers frequently listen to stories of psychological pain and traumatic events or watch loved ones struggle with intense emotional or behavioral issues. This repeated exposure can lead to STS, where caregivers begin to experience emotional duress similar to PTSD. Caregivers suffering from STS may exhibit signs such as increased anxiety, hypervigilance, emotional numbness, or intrusive thoughts. These symptoms not only mirror those of the primary trauma experienced by the individuals they care for but can also impact the caregiver's ability to function both professionally and personally. Caregivers who have personal histories of trauma, who lack adequate support, or who feel professionally isolated are at higher risk for developing STS.

All three conditions share some common symptoms, including sadness, apathy, irritability, insomnia, and various physical complaints. These issues not only affect caregivers' well-being but can also impede their ability to provide care effectively. Understanding and addressing these challenges are crucial for sustaining the mental health and well-being of caregivers in these roles.

Family and friends are often the ones who do the primary work to take care of someone with a significant mental health problem. They're often the ones who notice first if that person's behavior starts to change, so they're essential in helping them stay on track and get through tough times. This role is especially true for people with serious mental conditions like psychosis, who also might feel depressed or anxious, or people living with addiction. Even after periods of recovery or remission, the chances of facing a reoccurrence of these challenges can be high.

Caring for a loved one with chronic mental health issues is a profound commitment. Over time, continuous exposure to intense emotional situations and crises can lead to feelings of resentment and emotional numbness among caregivers. These reactions are common and understandable responses to the relentless demands of caregiving.

Resentment can surface when caregivers feel overwhelmed by the disproportionate share of responsibilities they bear, or when they perceive a lack of support from others. Resentment may also arise from sacrificing their own needs, desires, and aspirations to care for someone else. This feeling can be exacerbated by the loved one's seeming lack of progress or appreciation, or by the social isolation that often accompanies intensive caregiving roles.

Emotional numbness, or detachment, is a protective mechanism that caregivers may develop in response to ongoing stress. It serves as a way to cope with the intense emotions and constant demands placed on them. This numbness can manifest as a lack of empathy, diminished emotional response, or a general sense of disconnection from one's own feelings and from the person being cared for. It can be particularly distressing as it might make caregivers feel guilty or concerned about their seeming indifference to their loved one's suffering.

Mental health caregiving can significantly impact a caregiver's work life, negatively affecting performance, attendance, and overall job satisfaction. The effects are multifaceted and can lead to both short-term disruptions and long-term career consequences. The mental and emotional strain of caregiving responsibilities can lead to fatigue, stress, and distraction. This often results in decreased focus and productivity at work. Caregivers might need to take time off work frequently to deal with emergencies, attend medical appointments, or simply because they are too stressed or overwhelmed to work. This can lead to a higher rate of absenteeism, which can affect their reliability and the perception of their commitment to their job. Phone calls, texts, or the need to coordinate care during work hours can lead to frequent interruptions. These disruptions can affect a caregiver's ability to engage in sustained work activities or participate fully in meetings and other workplace functions. Some caregivers may find they need to make significant career sacrifices. This might include turning down promotions, not traveling for work, reducing working hours, or even quitting their job to manage caregiving responsibilities more effectively. The emotional toll of caregiving—such as stress, anxiety, and depression—can spill over into the workplace, affecting a caregiver's interactions with colleagues and superiors, and potentially leading to conflicts or misunderstandings.

One study[1] that explored the stress levels of people who take care of family members with mental health conditions found that roughly 32% of caregivers experienced high levels of stress because of their caregiving responsibilities. The researchers concluded that people who look after family members with mental health issues, especially in hospitals or dealing with psychotic symptoms, really need more targeted support. Additional research[2] confirms that looking after a loved one with a mental health condition is tough. Those who care for loved ones with these conditions often have a hard time themselves. They can get worn out physically, emotionally, and socially. Things like feeling left out from friends, money problems, job limitations, and a rollercoaster of feelings—from anger and frustration to worry and powerlessness—are common for these caregivers.

Looking after a family member with a serious mental health condition like schizophrenia, major depression, or bipolar disorder may lead to systemic family strain. One study looked at family members who provide this care without getting paid, whether they're the main caregivers or not. The participants talked about

1 Cham CQ, Ibrahim N, Siau CS, Kalaman CR, Ho MC, Yahya AN, Visvalingam U, Roslan S, Abd Rahman FN, Lee KW. Caregiver Burden among Caregivers of Patients with Mental Illness: A Systematic Review and Meta-Analysis. Healthcare (Basel). 2022 Nov 30;10(12):2423. doi: 10.3390/healthcare10122423. PMID: 36553947; PMCID: PMC9777672.
2 Rita Phillips, Mark Durkin, Hilary Engward, Graham Cable, Maria Iancu, The impact of caring for family members with mental illnesses on the caregiver: a scoping review, *Health Promotion International*, Volume 38, Issue 3, June 2023, daac049, https://doi.org/10.1093/heapro/daac049

"care burden" as the overall stress they felt, which can include dealing with emotional, physical, social, and money problems.[3]

Mental health caregivers often describe a feeling of "walking on eggshells," a metaphor that vividly captures the anxiety and tension of interacting with a loved one whose emotional state is highly volatile and unpredictable. This sensation stems from a deep-seated fear that saying or doing the wrong thing could precipitate a crisis, such as a suicidal episode. This emotional environment poses several challenges for caregivers. Caregivers may constantly worry about triggering a negative reaction. This persistent anxiety can be exhausting and debilitating, affecting the caregiver's own mental health. Being in a state of continuous alertness to monitor and respond to any sign of emotional distress can lead caregivers to feel overwhelmed and physically drained. The intense fear of causing harm can lead caregivers to feel paralyzed when making decisions, even those related to everyday activities or necessary confrontations about treatment and care.

Caregivers of people with chronic and severe mental health conditions often feel extra lonely and don't have much free time. They can be highly distressed because they must manage difficult situations like sudden angry outbursts or criticism from their loved one.

It takes a lot of resilience to care for someone with mental health challenges, but the caregiving role can also build resilience. Caregivers often develop the ability to keep going and even thrive

---

[3] Cheng, W.L., Chang, C.C., Griffiths, M.D. et al. Quality of life and care burden among family caregivers of people with severe mental illness: mediating effects of self-esteem and psychological distress. BMC Psychiatry 22, 672 (2022). https://doi.org/10.1186/s12888-022-04289-0

through tough times. It's not just about making it through the hard days, but also coming out stronger and more adaptable.

Quality of life (QoL) is critical for these caregivers. It's all about how they see their lives in the context of their own goals, standards, and worries, and it covers areas like physical health, mental well-being, social life, and having a supportive environment. If a caregiver's QoL isn't great, it can affect the whole family, including the person with the mental illness.

Previous studies have shown that caregivers of people with mental illness often have a lower QoL compared to the general population. Factors like how severe the illness is, especially if there are serious symptoms or behaviors like violence or suicidal actions, can make the caregiver's burden heavier and decrease their QoL.

Caregivers' own backgrounds can also affect their QoL. There's some debate about whether older caregivers have a worse QoL, but generally, women and parents, especially of people with schizophrenia, have a tougher time. Things like having less money, lower education, or not having a job can also make life harder for caregivers.

Caregivers' own feelings, like how they view themselves and their stress levels, can shape their QoL.

The Trials and Tribulations of Recovery, and Anticipatory Trauma and Grief

In the years that followed Carson's death, a haunting question lingered, whispering through the corridors of my mind: "Who is next?"

In 2013, graduation caps flew through the air. Hugs and tears and pride washed over us. Such a moment of achievement. Little did we know, another beloved relative—the graduate of that day (I will call him James)—had escalated from recreational Percocet use to heroin addiction. So much promise, so much devastation.

As James' addiction worsened over the next 18 months from that celebratory day, I felt increasingly powerless, especially being thousands of miles away. Soon he was shooting up daily, involved with gangs, and homeless.

The situation became so dire, I flew to see him, armed with resources and strategies for intervention shared by friends in long-term recovery. We gathered friends and family, who all expressed our love and concern, hoping to convince him to come home with me for treatment. Unfortunately, he wasn't ready to take that step, and I had to return home alone, heartbroken, sitting next to an empty seat.

His struggle with addiction continued to escalate until I visited him again, fearing it might be for the last time. We spent normal, everyday moments together—watching a movie, enjoying ice cream—and during these moments, I asked him to imagine the ideal future. All he could picture was a simple scene of peace on a beach. Remarkably, this small glimmer of hope and vision helped pave the way for the eventual first step into recovery. He managed to break free from heroin and moved closer to the coast, starting a new chapter of his life.

After five years of sobriety and a life that seemed to be on an upward trajectory—financial independence, physical fitness, and the joyful expectation of a first child—James faced a series of intense stressors. These challenges overwhelmed his coping mechanisms, leading to a reuse of opioids.

The journey of recovery from addiction is often fraught with both profound challenges and moments of hope, shaping the relationship between the person battling addiction and their supporter. This was true for us. Initially, my role was filled with optimism and encouragement as I witnessed strides toward sobriety. This phase strengthened our bond, filled with successes and a hopeful outlook.

The re-emergence of opioid use marked a pivotal moment, altering the dynamics between us. Where once we celebrated the victories, we now navigated a landscape of fear and disappointment. The fear of overdose became a persistent shadow, a relentless concern. I would send him information on recovery treatment centers and where to get Narcan. I had fentanyl test strips mailed to his home.

For me, this ongoing battle evoked a complex mix of emotions—fear and helplessness over the potential for loss, and hope inspired by my loved one's continued vision to overcome their dependency. Unconditional love, no matter what, as we rode the emotional rollercoaster together—reuse and resilience.

Ultimately, the journey through addiction recovery reshaped our relationship in profound ways, teaching both James and me about vulnerability, the strength of the human spirit, and the complex nature of hope and fear intertwined. Sometimes I would try to provide stability and positivity; other times I would manage personal feelings of anxiety and inadequacy.

Anticipatory trauma stalked me, a constant vigilance for signs of another storm on the horizon, another loved one to lose, another phone call that could shatter the fragile veneer of normalcy.

The fear is a relentless undercurrent, a reminder of past griefs and potential futures best left unimagined. Each day since Carson's departure, I walk a tightrope of tension, balancing between hope and the hard-learned understanding that sometimes, despite all love and vigilance, we are powerless to stop another's descent into darkness.

As a caregiver, you brace for impact with every interaction, knowing the terrain of mental illness is treacherous and unpredictable.

Mental health caregivers who support loved ones dealing with severe mental health issues such as addiction or tendencies toward self-harm can experience a specific type of stress known as anticipatory trauma. This form of psychological stress is rooted in the ongoing fear and anticipation of a possible tragic event involving the person they care for such as suicide, overdose, or other self-inflicted harm.

Caregivers might even experience anticipatory sadness, fear, anger, and helplessness as they foresee the loss of their loved one to suicide, overdose, or the consequences of addiction. This involves the caregiver mentally and emotionally preparing for the death of their loved one. It includes imagining life without the person and potentially detaching emotionally to protect themselves from the full impact of the actual loss.

These feelings can be intense and fluctuate widely as the caregiver grapples with the impending changes and ultimate loss. Anticipatory trauma sometimes manifests due to the caregiver's constant vigilance and the hyper-awareness of potential signs of crisis. At the worst of it, I found myself on edge with heightened worry followed by detachment and numbness, feeling helpless.

Recovery is never a straight path, and reusing is often a part of the journey. Today, James is able to provide for his family while maintaining an active addiction. He is more afraid of the withdrawal and losing work than he is enjoying any pleasurable experience of being high. Ours is an ongoing story, and I have tried to learn the patience needed in supporting a loved one through this process. For those of us supporting someone in recovery, it's about maintaining hope and staying engaged, even when the path forward seems uncertain.

Sustaining Strength: Empowering Mental Health Caregivers to Confront Compassion Fatigue, Burnout, and Secondary Trauma

Self-Reflection

When we ask ourselves the following questions, we help ourselves assess our well-being, effectiveness, and sustainability. Here are some thought-provoking questions that mental health caregivers, both professional and unpaid, might consider:

1. Am I taking care of my own mental and physical health? Am I tending to my soul care?
2. Have I set clear boundaries, and am I maintaining them?
3. What emotions am I suppressing, and what are they telling me about my needs?

4. How has my relationship with the person I care for changed, and how do I feel about these changes?
5. Am I experiencing feelings of guilt or inadequacy, and where do these feelings come from?
6. What are my sources of support, and am I utilizing them effectively?
7. Am I allowing the person I care for to maintain as much independence as possible?
8. How do I handle feelings of resentment or anger toward the person I'm caring for?
9. What joys and rewards do I experience in caregiving?
10. How do I see my role evolving, and am I prepared for future changes?

Peer Support and Coping Skills

Social support in particular plays a significant role in mitigating the mental health risks associated with caregiving for someone living with a mental health condition. Feeling connected to others helps combat the loneliness and isolation that can lead to depression among caregivers. Support groups, where caregivers can connect with others facing similar challenges, have proven especially beneficial. These groups provide a sense of community and allow caregivers to share experiences and strategies, which can make managing care responsibilities less overwhelming.

For instance, the National Alliance on Mental Illness (NAMI) Family-to-Family program is a free educational course specifically designed for family members, significant others, and friends of people with mental health conditions facilitated by peers who have firsthand experience. Recognized as an evidence-based program, it offers a structured group that aims to improve the coping and problem-solving abilities of participants. The program provides critical information on a wide array of mental illnesses and their impact on the person affected and their family. Participants learn strategies for personal and emotional self-care as well as ways to handle the complexities of mental illness, including enhanced communication techniques that can help facilitate more effective interaction with the person under care, thereby improving empathy and collaborative problem-solving. The Family-to-Family group also provides an opportunity to meet others in similar situations, creating a support network.

Help for the Helper and Soul Care[4]

Caregivers might find they need to seek help in the form of therapy or respite care. Sometimes caregivers need professional coaching to establish clear boundaries about what they are willing and able to do. Professionals can also help the caregiver develop a collaborative crisis response plan with the person they are supporting. Having a plan in place for managing acute crises, such as potential suicide attempts, can reduce anxiety by preparing caregivers to respond effectively in emergency situations. I know for me, getting support from my peers in long term recovery was essential in finding hope in our situation.

---

4   Gaer, S. (2023) Soul Exhaustion and Forgiveness https://youtu.be/K3wCr0dJij4?si=0O6hv8J5jWbgLAFX.

Self-care and soul care, while overlapping, cater to different aspects of a person's well-being, especially for those in the mentally taxing role of caregiving. Self-care typically refers to activities and practices that maintain one's physical health and emotional stability. This includes eating well, getting enough sleep, exercising, engaging in hobbies, and taking breaks when needed. Self-care is often the first line of defense against stress and burnout for mental health caregivers. I have found that walking my dogs in the predawn darkness gives me a sense of peace and connects me to something bigger than myself. When I get home, I feel a little more empowered, and little more hopeful.

Soul care delves deeper. It addresses the spiritual or existential depletion that can occur in demanding emotional roles—a phenomenon that might be termed "soul exhaustion." Soul care is about nourishing the essence of who you are. It goes beyond the physical and mental to revitalize one's sense of purpose, connection, and inner peace. Practices might include meditation, prayer, deep personal reflection, engaging in meaningful and joyful activities, and nurturing relationships that affirm one's sense of self. For my soul care, I have found it important to advocate for overdose prevention in the community—to turn my ongoing pain into purpose. I also strive to continue to show up in a meaningful way for James and his growing family. He is more than his addiction.

For mental health caregivers, who are often absorbed in the emotional and psychological trials of those they support, soul care is crucial for long-term well-being. It's not just about staying physically healthy and emotionally balanced, but also about sustaining the inner vitality that fuels compassion and empathy. Without soul care, caregivers may find that their ability to connect with others, to feel hope and joy, and to maintain their own identity becomes diminished. Caregiving, particularly in the mental health field, can involve witnessing profound suffering and taking on heavy emotional loads, which can erode one's sense of self. Soul care embodies the "five Rs":

- **Replenish Inner Strength**
  It replenishes the inner resources that can be drained by the intensity of caregiving.
- **Restore Identity**
  Caregivers often put their own needs and identities aside. Soul care helps them reconnect with who they are beyond their caregiver role.
- **Reaffirm Purpose**
  It helps to reaffirm a sense of purpose, which can be especially important in facing the challenges and stresses of caregiving.
- **Renew Sense of Hope**
  Engaging in soul care can reignite the sense of hope and optimism that can be worn down by constant exposure to others' pain.
- **Revitalize Compassion**
  It ensures that the caregiver's capacity for compassion is not just maintained but deepened, allowing them to give of themselves without becoming depleted.

In essence, while self-care keeps a caregiver functioning, soul care keeps them feeling alive, whole, and connected to their essence. It's an essential, though often overlooked, aspect of sustaining the ability to provide compassionate and effective care over the long term.

Acknowledging the full spectrum of the caregiving experience has been essential for me. Ultimately, mental health caregiving is a testament to the complexity of the human spirit, its capacity for boundless love, and its need for self-preservation.

.

Snowy Egret Takes Flight

Richa Chadha, MBA, MS

Richa is a Mindset Coach, speaker, and organizational psychologist based in the Bay Area, California. With an MBA and a degree in Organizational Dynamics from UPenn, she brings nearly a decade of experience in the banking and finance sector, managing cross-cultural teams. Richa likes to call herself a global citizen; she loves to travel and immerse herself in local cultures. She and her equally adventurous husband have journeyed across six continents and explored more than half of the United States. Inspired by her own experience of re-establishing herself in the U.S. after moving from India, Richa is passionate about continuous learning and personal growth. Through her venture, Coachampion, she helps leaders and teams transform their mindset from "Why me?" to "Watch me rise." Connect with her at coachampion.com or by email at richa@coachampion.com, and join her mental wellness community on Instagram at @coachampion_richachadha.

Richa Chadha, MBA, MS

From Duty to Choice: Navigating Cultural Expectations

Part 1: India

In Indian culture, family and community bonds are strong, with a deep-rooted tradition of caring for others. Our society is mostly patriarchal, and women often take on caregiving roles, whether for children, elderly relatives, or even extended family members. This extends to professional settings, too, with many women working in fields like health care, social work, and education.

Although my family never imposed these expectations on me, I absorbed them from society and from watching women like my mother, who sacrificed personal desires to care for their husbands and children. Despite this, I grew up to be an independent woman (at least in my mind) who always thought of others before making any decision for herself. Quite paradoxical!

I've faced many moments in life that brought on compassion fatigue, but through awareness and learning how to cope, I'm now able to prioritize caring for myself. This journey has shaped me into the kind and caring person I am today. The big difference? I make sure to shower myself with that care and kindness first.

I've seen so many women in my life, like my mom, aunts, and grandmother, work tirelessly from early morning until late at night, almost like machines for the family, without taking a moment for themselves. My mom's typical day started with cleaning the house, making our favorite breakfast, packing lunches for my brother and me, and sending us off to school. Then she'd rush to the kitchen to prepare lunch for my dad, who ate early and left for work around 10 a.m.

By the time my mom got a little free time in the afternoon for her hobbies, like knitting (usually sweaters or scarves for us, never for herself) or sewing, we'd be back from school. Her afternoons were all about helping us with schoolwork, homework, and our activities. We'd often take a nap together, but I remember waking her up with our quarrels. Looking back, I feel terrible for taking even those few moments of rest away from her.

In the evenings, my mom focused on meals, helping us with our studies, and preparing for the next school day. The day would usually end with her cooking and serving dinner to the family. This routine has been followed by her and many other women I know for decades. They haven't complained, taken breaks, or asked for help in years. However, there's one common thread: they've all experienced compassion fatigue. I can tell because I see signs of resentment, apathy, overwhelm, and exhaustion. I often wonder how deeply ingrained the conditioning is that leads these women to give all of themselves for their families.

While I haven't closely followed the lives of all these women, I've observed my mother closely. She's a gifted singer who used to pursue music before getting married, dreaming of a professional career. Fast forward 38 years, she still sings while cooking for us and records songs on her cellphone to share when we're away. This is just one of the sacrifices she's made for us. She's also endured numerous health issues and mental and physical struggles simply because she's a woman in a society that expects such sacrifices based on gender alone.

Honestly, I never really noticed my mother's sacrifices because I thought that's just what moms or married women did. It only hit me after I got married! Suddenly, my whole world and perspective shifted. I began feeling the weight of responsibilities I hadn't even realized existed. Years of conditioning had played a role. I felt overwhelmed, trying to balance household chores, work, and my own dreams. Even though both my husband and I were working, I took on the responsibility of making sure breakfast was ready on time (thankfully, we had domestic help), lunches were packed, dinner was prepared before we got home from work, and clothes were ironed for the next day. Somehow, I was always the one my cook would call to ask about dinner plans. There were even times when, while in a serious meeting with my bosses, I'd answer the phone to tell her to cook dal (lentils) and roti (chapati/bread). My husband never got those calls!

The pandemic was incredibly stressful for everyone, but for millions of Indian women like me working as frontline workers, it was even more overwhelming. I had to report to my workplace and work for 12 hours every day, and once I got home, I would get to cooking, cleaning, and taking care of the family. Mornings were especially tough with the added pressure of preparing breakfast and lunch before heading out. Before the pandemic, our cook helped with these tasks, but since outsiders were no longer allowed into our community, the burden fell on us women, automatically.

At work, while we were all struggling to keep up, I remember some older men coming in just to chat because they were bored at home. This made my job tougher because I had to go home to an asthmatic husband. Those moments made me realize how unaware some people were of the impact they were having on others. The burden of all the added physical and mental work made me feel trapped with no way out. Sleep was restless, leaving me more tired than before. Emotionally, I felt like a frayed wire, ready to snap under pressure. Physically, the tension coiled in my muscles, refusing to let go. Recognizing the toll compassion fatigue was taking on me was the first step toward healing and self-discovery.

The problem with a society like ours is that while we've become modern on paper in many ways, the mindset hasn't fully evolved. Women have become ambitious and career-oriented, moving beyond traditional roles, yet the burden of household responsibilities still falls on women. They often feel guilty for not dedicating enough time to their home, in-laws, or children.

Well, perhaps even the gods admired my resilience, as the pandemic eventually came to an end and the lockdown lifted. We were able to live and breathe again. Life was slowly returning to normal; then came the news of my husband's acceptance to MIT Sloan for his MBA—a major achievement. So we decided to move to Boston, USA. This was a joyous moment for both of us. I was of course happy, but something was dragging me down. The thought of moving so far away from my loved ones felt like leaving a part of myself behind. I almost felt like leaving my "kids" behind (by that I mean my parents and my 30-year-old brother, for who all I did so much). I fretted over who would care for them while I was away.

Surprisingly, no one else seemed to share my worries, not even the people I was worried about. Instead, they all rallied behind me, urging me to seize this opportunity and even pursue my dream of earning a second master's degree. When I told my dad, "I can't go. Who'll take care of you and Mom?" he replied, "Beta (child), you need to take care of yourself and stop worrying about us. Go seize all the new opportunities life is presenting to you, and we'll be happy."

It all felt a bit surreal, like nobody really understood the depth of my emotions. Tears welled up on the flight to the United States as I embarked on this new chapter of my life.

Part 2: The United States

Moving to the United States marked the beginning of a pivotal phase in my life. Here, I liberated myself from a multitude of self-limiting beliefs, societal expectations, and the burden of unnecessary responsibilities. I came to understand that it wasn't my duty to worry about everyone, care for everyone, and constantly sacrifice my own well-being for the sake of others.

Now, the US didn't magically cure me of these burdens. It was the result of at least two years of hard work (literally... we could not afford domestic help here!). I persevered and toiled until I found my way into collaborating with professors and engaging in their groundbreaking research at Sloan. Immersing myself in the field of organizational psychology, a passion I had always harbored, became my focus. During my MBA days, I fell in love with the subject of organizational psychology, and now, given the opportunity to delve into it further, there was no way I was going to pass it up.

Despite some internal (and plenty of external) pressure to seek employment at a bank, I ultimately chose not to pursue that route. This was the first step to realizing that I could make my own decisions and say no to things that didn't serve me. Being financially independent brought a sense of joy and freedom that I only truly appreciated during this period of unemployment. Though I never imagined I'd have to relinquish it, perhaps it was a small price to pay for the opportunity to rediscover myself.

I used to work for more than 12 hours a day at my last job. I found myself doing the same here—cooking, cleaning, and immersing myself in research work. The only difference was that here, I wasn't getting paid for any of it. Also, I never expected my husband to contribute much at home since he was busy at school, and I thought of this as my job to keep the household running.

Because I was incredibly passionate about creating healthier, less toxic workplaces and raising awareness about mental health,

I devoured countless books and research papers, and I enrolled in various psychology and coaching courses. Eventually, I completed my coaching training, accumulated over 500 coaching hours, passed the exam, and became a certified professional coach and a team coach.

But that wasn't all. I finally mustered the courage to apply for my master's in organizational dynamics at UPenn, and to my delight, I was accepted! The joy I felt was boundless, and my mother was over the moon. Seeing me pursue dreams that I had long buried made her realize that I was charting a different path—one where I didn't sacrifice myself and my aspirations for the sake of others, as she had done. I remember my mom telling me, "I'm proud of you for choosing to live life on your own terms. Never forget to prioritize your happiness." I wish she had done it, too.

This dream—to pursue my second master's (I already have an MBA) in a field I deeply care about, Organizational Psychology—from an Ivy League school, felt like the ultimate triumph. And when my thirty-year-old "baby" brother assured me that they no longer needed me to take care of them and encouraged me to live my life to the fullest, I felt an overwhelming sense of gratitude.

Old habits indeed have a way of sticking around, and I was living proof of that. Despite making progress in prioritizing my own needs, I still found myself falling back into my old patterns of caring for others at the expense of my own well-being. I juggled multiple roles as a student, a full-time homemaker, entrepreneur, and above all, an exhaustingly caring individual.

Even though I had begun to recognize the importance of self-care, there were still moments when I placed others' needs ahead of my own. I would even go so far as to maintain kindness towards those who weren't particularly kind to me. I vividly remember a friend's visit; although our relationship wasn't the warmest, I went out of my way to ensure their comfort during their stay. I cooked for them, showed them around, and endured discomfort to make their visit as pleasant as possible without even getting a benign thank-you in return. Looking back, I often wondered why I felt compelled to act in this way.

I took a hard look at my life, like a banker checking accounts. One day, feeling overwhelmed, I decided to take a walk along the Charles River in Cambridge. As I walked, the sound of leaves and the gentle flow of the river created a calming effect. The crisp air smelled of fresh grass and coffee from nearby cafes. Sunlight sparkled on the water, and I watched rowers glide by while students laughed and picnicked. With each step, my stress started to fade, and I felt clearer. Being by the river and seeing the students' joy made me realize I had been neglecting my own well-being. I understood that self-care wasn't selfish—it was necessary. This peaceful walk reminded me to take care of myself and dial down the need to take care of everything and everyone around me.

Through this process, I came to a significant realization: I had been continuously giving and showering kindness on individuals who overlooked or took advantage of me. This realization served as a tipping point for me to reevaluate my approach. I delved deeper into self-reflection and adopted these simple yet impactful practices to gain more awareness.

How I Supported Myself

Nurturing My Inner Resilience

I began prioritizing my well-being and values above all else. This involved embracing meditation and yoga practices, which proved instrumental in healing my mind, body, and soul. As I embarked on this journey of self-recovery, I also made a conscious effort to distance myself from negative influences in my life. Whether they came in the form of people, activities, or discussions, I became increasingly discerning about what and who I allowed into my life.

Despite my best efforts, these negative forces sometimes still found their way in. In such instances, I developed a relaxation technique centered around deep breathing. If discomfort persisted, I found the courage to confront the person or situation directly and unapologetically. I stopped prioritizing others' feelings over my own and began advocating for myself and my values. This newfound assertiveness allowed me to set boundaries that protected my well-being and upheld my principles.

Creating a Circle of Strength

After relocating to the US, I had drifted away from my friends and extended family. I made a conscious effort to reconnect with them while also forging new, meaningful connections. Reconnecting with old friends provided me with an outlet and allowed me to immerse myself in their worlds, which had a profound psychological impact on me.

Additionally, I began seeking professional support when needed. Engaging with therapists or coaches became a regular part of my routine. With their guidance, I made significant progress that I was truly proud of. The days no longer felt monotonous and burdensome; I realized that I had the power to shape each day as I desired. The weight of unnecessary responsibilities and chores gradually lifted, allowing me to reclaim a sense of control over my life.

Fortifying My Inner Boundaries

I created a clear routine that balanced my professional commitments with activities that nourished my soul. This included taking leisurely walks in nature, engaging with plants and trees, striking up conversations with strangers, assisting those in need, learning a new language, meeting up with friends, and treating myself to solo coffee dates. Learning to say no was a significant challenge that required practice, but I'm pleased to say that I've made substantial progress in this area. This newfound assertiveness not only empowered me to set boundaries with others but also taught me the importance of saying no to myself when I found myself compromising my own well-being.

Commitment to Lifelong Growth

I've remained committed to learning more about myself, my life, and the intricacies of our brain functions. This commitment has led me to attend numerous workshops and training sessions focused on stress management, self-care, and resilience, recognizing these as invaluable investments in my personal growth.

Additionally, I make it a point to indulge in reading every night before bed. These books often delve into general psychology or topics that pique my curiosity, providing me with ongoing enrichment and insight.

Mastering the Art of Self-Reflection

I discovered that the concept of reflection extends far beyond merely looking at oneself in the mirror. During my coaching training, I was introduced to the idea of starting a reflection practice, and although I initially hesitated, I gradually embraced it and continued to build upon it.

Journaling has become a cherished practice for me, providing a space to release my feelings and process my emotions. This outlet has been instrumental in preventing emotional outbursts, allowing me to navigate triggers with greater ease. In addition to journaling, I dedicate time to introspection, engaging in conversations with myself about my experiences and emotions. This introspective dialogue helps me understand my actions and reactions, explore ways to handle my emotions more effectively, and view them as sources of strength rather than obstacles.

This practice of self-reflection has become my favorite and is one that I wholeheartedly recommend. Whether it's embarking on a solo trip or taking that dance class you've been eyeing, or even doing nothing and spending time alone with your thoughts, it can be incredibly rewarding. Embrace your own company—you'll be amazed at the insights you discover.

Living with Presence and Appreciation

I used to pride myself on multitasking, believing it to be a superpower. Little did I know, it was causing more harm than good. I found myself becoming increasingly unfocused, with a diminished attention span and a constant sense of burnout. However, through self-exploration, I discovered the profound benefits of mindfulness and the power of focusing on one task at a time.

As I began practicing mindfulness, I noticed a remarkable transformation within myself. I became a calmer individual, more attentive, with improved memory, better sleep quality, and significantly reduced stress and anxiety. Alongside mindfulness, I cultivated the practice of gratitude, recognizing the countless blessings in my life. I realized that it all comes down to focus: When you focus on the negatives, you see them everywhere, leading to dissatisfaction and distress. But when you shift your focus to gratitude, you begin to see blessings manifesting all around you. This shift in perspective cultivates mental peace, a positive outlook on life, and the ability to find beauty even in the most challenging circumstances.

Part 3: Life Now

I recognize how fortunate I am to have gained this awareness, as it's a struggle for many individuals. My journey has equipped me with the tools and insights to navigate compassion fatigue, and now I'm committed to making life easier for others facing similar challenges. It's a mission close to my heart, and my first student had to be none other than my own mother!

Having heartfelt conversations with my mother wasn't easy; it required courage and patience to gently make her realize that she had been neglecting the most important person in her life: herself. At one point, I was urging her, "Mom, you really need to take better care of yourself, loosen up a bit and stop putting everyone else before your own well-being." Her innocent response was, "But then who will take care of all of you?" I was momentarily at a loss for words. Before I could respond, she excitedly interrupted, "Guess what? I made your favorite dessert, want to try some?" That's just the way moms are, always putting others first. As someone without kids myself, I'm still figuring it all out!

Despite the initial resistance, she eventually embraced my perspective and decided to give my approach a chance. She understood that prioritizing her well-being did not mean neglecting everybody else's. The transformation in her life has been extraordinary. She now recognizes that she has the power to prioritize herself and her needs while still being kind and caring.

I was overjoyed to learn that she joined a music class recently, reigniting her passion for melody and song. Additionally, she delved into spiritual practices, finding solace and fulfillment amidst her responsibilities as a wife and mother. The radiant glow of inner happiness on her face speaks volumes, far surpassing the effects of any expensive makeup. Her newfound contentment has inspired her to extend a helping hand to other women, orphans, and the underprivileged. Despite being busier than ever, she radiates a sense of fulfillment and satisfaction that she's never experienced before.

I've made it a personal mission to share my journey of overcoming compassion fatigue with others, offering the insights I gained after 35 years of prioritizing others over myself. I firmly believe in providing support to those who may not have had the same opportunities for growth and healing that I did. So, I will do what I do best: create awareness, talk to people, and support them in navigating their challenges with strength and resilience.

Saying "no" can be a powerful act of kindness—not only to myself but also to others. By setting clear boundaries, I wasn't just protecting my own well-being; I was also nurturing healthier, more respectful relationships.

Compassion fatigue isn't a sign of weakness but a natural response to prolonged exposure to emotional stress. I used to think feeling drained meant I was weak. Realizing that it's a common experience among caring individuals allowed me to approach it with compassion for myself and to seek ways to manage it, rather than feeling ashamed or inadequate.

Support systems are not just a backup; they are essential. Reaching out for help, reconnecting with old friends, and building new relationships provided me with strength and resilience I never knew I had. Vulnerability can be a source of strength.

The conventional wisdom often emphasizes productivity and constant striving. But by embracing mindfulness and gratitude, I learned to slow down, appreciate the present moment, and find joy in the simple things.

I now see that taking care of myself is not a detour from my path of helping others but a critical part of it. I invite you to reconsider your own beliefs about self-care and compassion. Challenge the notion that you must sacrifice your well-being to care for others. Embrace the idea that by nurturing yourself, you are enhancing your capacity to make a positive impact in the world. Also, men in our society need to understand that nobody cooks *for her*, cleans *for her*, or cares *for her*. We, as a system need to take a pledge to stop expecting women to sacrifice themselves in order to take care of everyone else.

Hello, Sunflower

Antoinette LeCouteur

Antoinette is an author, publisher, philanthropy advisor, and caregiver who is driven to help people do good in the world. A theatre major in college and actor early in her career, she transitioned to the world of philanthropy and social impact in the mid-2000s and has helped get hundreds of millions of dollars in employee donations and corporate funds to charities all over the world. Her photography, which can be seen in the books *Together* and *Twist*, captures reality as it happens, documenting the unstaged world in its most authentic state, showing unique moments from new angles. She is part of the Gray Bear Publications leadership team. Contact her at antoinette@graybearpublications.com or on Instagram at @sf_antoinette.

Antoinette LeCouteur

When She is Gone, We Will Still be a Family

When the phone call came in February of 2022, I had no idea how much my life would be changed by a simple fall or how resilient my family could be. My sister called to tell me that our 87-year-old mother had fallen and broken her hip. Through the tears and exhaustion, my sister shared what she knew. Mom had fallen sometime the day before and spent hours on the floor before she finally dragged herself to her cell phone and called my sister late that night.

My sister and niece arrived to find my mom alert, with no obvious injuries. She just couldn't move without pain. Mom was sure she only had a bad bruise and could simply sleep it off. Anyone who has met my mother knows she can be very convincing, so because they couldn't move her, they gave her a blanket and decided to spend the night and see how she would feel in the morning. Humans are not good self-reporters, and as caregivers we learn you can't always believe the patient even if they're saying what you hope to hear.

None of them imagined she was truly injured, but when she still couldn't stand in the morning, they called 911. The paramedics felt it was likely she had broken something, so they took her to emergency. An x-ray confirmed she had a clean break in her hip, and they scheduled surgery later that day. The doctors said they would get her moving, and once she could walk, she'd be discharged. We all assumed that meant a week or so in a rehabilitation facility, and we'd have time to figure out how we would support her at home.

The next day, when my sister went to visit my mom, she was met by a very compassionate nurse with a stack of paperwork and instructions on how to access home health care. The nurse said that since mom had family and no chronic health issues, she would be sent home… tomorrow! My sister, whose Parkinson's symptoms were being flared by all the stress and lack of sleep, called me again. She was somewhat frantic because not only were they not sending her to rehab, but tomorrow was Friday so home health care wouldn't start until Monday. She and my nieces would need to care for our mom until I arrived.

Our family had been thrust into an all-too-common story: ill-prepared, in denial, working adult children caring for an aging parent in a crisis. As my sister, through tears and fatigue, relayed what was happening, I realized my role as a part-time caregiver living 600 miles away was over. After we hung up, I turned to my partner, who hugged me close and said calmly, I think you need to go there now. I had no time to consider what I would do about my work, my commitments, or just how many ways my life would change. I just knew my family needed my help. So, within 72 hours of my mother's fall, I was on a plane and launched into the role of full-time caregiver.

When I last visited my mom, she was cooking her own meals, managing her personal care, and had no health issues at all. She had lived alone for more years than she had with people, she was fiercely independent, she had minimal experience with trauma, and she disliked taking medication and asking for help.

When I arrived, I walked through the door to find my exhausted sister still reeling from the trauma of finding our mother. She had retained only part of the nurse's instructions and was mostly working from instinct. My mother was terrified. She hadn't spent any time in a hospital in her whole life, other than giving birth to her children. The shock of what had happened really hadn't worn off yet, and she was heavily medicated. My sister tried to pass along what she could and then went home to sleep.

I had no idea what providing this level of care would be like until I was doing it. I had chosen not to have children, so being in charge of someone else's basic needs—let alone managing a resistant patient—was something I did not have much experience with. And of course, the patient is my mom, so the added layer of family expectations and hierarchy was very real. I naively thought, *It will be a few days and then we will have full time care. I can do this.*

But in fact home health is rarely 24/7 care, and what I thought would be a few days of intensive care became weeks of doing almost everything for her, from daily care needs to nagging and fighting with her to do her physical therapy and take her medication. Because I was here and in the thick of it, I also took on all the admin work: insurance claims, finances, and medical appointments. Anyone who's done this knows that all this is a full-time job. I was in crisis mode the whole time, jumping from one task to the next and constantly adding new items to the must-do list. It felt easier to just do it all myself than to figure out how anyone else could help. And, even when they offered or I did manage to give them something to do, I would have to resist judging it as incomplete or something I would just have to fix later. I did some self-care—often prescribed to caregivers—which was easier said than done. I went for walks when the home health aides were here, or my sister or nieces would come over to visit. I tried to eat well and not drink too much, but honestly when I was in that crisis mindset, I really couldn't think of anything but getting stuff done and how much the endless sense of urgency and stress was building up. My lifeline was daily calls and texts with my partner, who is a professional coach and helped me to stay focused and balanced. These calls and his support were the basis on which I built my care plan and strengthened our family's resilience.

I also made an effort to be honest about everything with my sisters. One was physically close by and the other lived a state away, but if one of us was going to move in and live with Mom, I was the obvious choice both in job flexibility and physical capability. As the youngest, I was the only one who had lived with her alone. They were both very grateful and would often say that despite having raised kids, they didn't think they could have done what I did.

The other big worry was money. Our mother had worked hard her whole life, but since her retirement we had all been contributing to her support in one way or another. Her social security and small retirement fund were all she had, and that wouldn't last long if we had to pay for care. I am self-employed, so that meant I had the flexibility to come for the short term, but it also meant I wasn't getting paid and had no family leave coverage. I could pretend that having no income was okay for a while, but as weeks turned into months the money stress became one more worry weighing on me. I thought a lot about how it wasn't reasonable for me to stop working to be her caregiver long term, and my sisters agreed. The question was: how could we avoid it.

My mother was not what you would call a good patient. She can be very charming and put on a good face for the professionals, but when they left, she would slide back into fear and refusing care.

Despite having to take care of all her daily needs, nag her to take her medication and do her exercise, navigate all the healthcare and government systems, and research housing and financial options, I would say the hardest part was helping her to process everything emotionally. She repeated stories of past traumas, regrets, and her fears of the future. Some came with anger at the injustice of it all, and others were shame-filled confessions. I slept in the room next to hers and kept the door open so I could hear her whenever she got up. This also meant that I heard every scream, every moan, and every sob as she often had nightmares. I learned later that falls in the elderly can trigger something similar to PTSD, but at the time it just felt like my strong and capable mother was unraveling before my very eyes. And as I laid in the dark listening to her voice filled with fear and regret, I would find myself wishing it would just end.

Seeing your parent turn into a frightened and anxious human is not easy, and while I did my best to endure it, I didn't truly appreciate how much of a toll it took on me until months later. I spoke to several friends who shared their experience caring for their parents, listening to me without judgment and making me feel less alone. When I finally found a support group to join, I thought, *Now I will be with people who get it and will have answers.* I hoped that they would help me identify what was truly important and offer solutions. Unfortunately, it was anything but that.

The group I found was not an uplifting community but a place where people went to wallow, complain, and commiserate. It also made me realize that how I had been approaching this whole situation wasn't going to work long term. This support group gave me a full-color picture into just how bad it could get. I met one woman who had been caring for her mother with dementia for eight years, and after moving her mom in with her, she went broke and finally got sick herself, with, among other things, scurvy! She had recently moved her mother into a care facility and was now able to focus on her own health, but she wasn't sure she'd ever be able to go back to work again. She was only 46 years old. Now she just puts up with her mom calling 10 times a day to accuse her of being a bad daughter or cry and beg her to take her home.

There were others who shared stories of wars with their siblings over money or care plans, and still others who had sacrificed their careers and marriages. Most were weary, lonely, and resentful. I would come off those calls and feel so grateful that my mother was as healthy as she was and that both my siblings were supportive and generous. I may have been on the front line for those few months, but I knew from listening to the other caregivers that we needed to make a plan that wasn't based on our roles in the family, or what society expected of us as daughters, but one we designed ourselves that would support us all. I also learned that we were beyond lucky that we genuinely liked each other and shared the same values. We all love our mother and want her to be safe and healthy, but it became clear to me that the most important relationships would be the ones we had as sisters, not the one we each had with our mother. The three of us would still be a family after our mother was gone, and it was that shift that helped me the most to move out of the overwhelm and into building a plan.

Despite all the emotional labor and physical demands, the part that really got to me was how fragmented and broken the system of health care and support truly is. The system's expectation was that because my mom had family, she would be better off at home and of course we would be her caregivers. The individuals who provided my mom's care were all professional, compassionate, and deeply committed to her care. Many gave me valuable advice on how to navigate the process, but they were also all burdened with working in a broken system. A system built to drive you into crisis before you get the help that you need. After that first fall, my mom should not have been sent home with my sister; she should have gone to rehab. No one asked if my sister was physically able to care for my mother, and no one asked about her Parkinson's even though it would have been hard to miss, given how exhausted she was. She was given little choice but to put her own and my mother's safety in jeopardy, as many family caregivers do. As I became aware of how our system is built on the expectation that millions of unpaid family caregivers must just step up and provide care regardless of what it costs them, it just added to my anger and stress. Ultimately, though, it also strengthened my resolve to find a way to manage our mother's care that would not risk anyone's health or make any of us go broke.

After two months, she had recovered physically and was stable enough for me to leave. We hired a home health aide to come three days a week, and my sister and nieces would manage the errands and appointments as they had before Mom fell.

    I was beyond tired. I couldn't really think about much other than getting back to California and my old life. Once I was home, I took a minute to catch my breath and realized we'd been given a preview and now had at least a small window where we could regroup and move from crisis management to preparing for what could—and would—happen next. There were so many questions. What happens if she falls again? What can we do to avoid it? Can she stay in the house—which she desperately wanted to do—or should we move her somewhere with more support? If we did, would they take her cats? What legal paperwork did we need to get in place? Who should be her power of attorney? How would we qualify her for Medicaid? How would we afford her care if she didn't?

I talked to anyone and everyone I met about their experience. I spent hours in webinars and caregiving calls. I read blogs and books, and I campaigned for family care legislation. After I felt like I had done the research, I decided I needed to invest in my own resilience. I found a new group to join, focused on self-compassion for caregivers[1]. I went through a coaching course in Positive Intelligence with my partner, where I improved my skills at managing my own actions both in a crisis and in everyday life. I learned about strengths-based skills and how to design a team that allows for everyone to contribute using their strengths. I thought about how to apply all this to my family and how to work collaboratively. I also strived to change my limiting beliefs about myself and my family. I focused less on what I thought I knew and reflected on how everyone had stepped up over the past year—especially my nieces, in supporting both their grandmother and their own mother. This crisis had matured them from teenagers to adults before my eyes, and by allowing them to contribute we were letting them improve their skills, too.

Our care plan was no longer just about responding to a single crisis, or based on one person doing a single task, but we were building it into one that would support us as a family regardless of what came next. It was focused on the future, reflected our commitment to each other, and ensured no one would be left to process the hard stuff alone. The main way I put all this into practice was by sharing what I learned about solutions in planning for our mother's future, and in continuing to be open about anything I was struggling with. We made most decisions around her care collectively.

---

1   self-compassion.org

We all agreed to keep each other apprised of anything we noticed as well as share anything our mother said about her health. She has been known to play us off each other, and she doesn't always tell the same story from one daughter to the next. So, when Mom complained to one sister that the professional caregiver was a waste of money and that she didn't need help and was going to fire her, that sister knew what to say without having to check in with the others. The three of us had already agreed that the caregiver was necessary, and we valued their feedback. What we didn't realize at the time was that Mom's behaviors were the early signs of dementia, and so as she got more aggressive or denied something we'd learned from the caregiver, we were able to trust the process and not question each other. Admittedly, it is very hard to unlearn family patterns so this took some practice, but we found that over time keeping each other in the loop kept our focus on the bigger goal of keeping Mom safe and healthy for as long as we could.

All that work we did as a family during the two years before her second fall made us so much more resilient. When she fell that second time, it was a challenge but not a crisis. We knew we were in it together; we knew we would be okay no matter what happened.

That second fall came almost two years to the day. We got lucky again because the housekeeper happened to arrive just a few minutes after she fell. When my mom didn't answer the door, the housekeeper came around back and saw mom lying on the floor. She let herself in, called 911, then called my niece from mom's emergency contacts and waited till the paramedics arrived. A friend later suggested that if she'd had a life alert button or smart speaker, she could have helped herself. The truth is my mom—again—didn't think she was hurt. So, like many people do when they fall, she might have denied she was hurt because she wouldn't want to be a burden or have an emergency room visit cost too much money. Humans are not good judges of our own predicament, and while there are a lot of advancements in fall-detection technology and aging-in-place design, it is not foolproof. I am just glad that despite making some safety improvements in her house and her lifestyle, we all understood there were limits. We had agreed to strike a balance between her desire for independence and keeping her safe, and so we were emotionally prepared to accept what came next.

That fall broke her tailbone, and she was sent to a rehabilitation center to heal as there was no surgical option. We managed to take turns bringing her food, keeping her company, and cheering her on in rehab. Several members of the staff told us how nice it was for Mom to have such a strong family that worked together so well.

The pain subsided, but she still struggled a lot. She was paranoid the staff were out to get her, and she had delusions of how she had been put in that facility to keep her quiet. Her mood would swing from enthusiastically doing her physical therapy one day, to shouting rude insults at the staff the next. We were sure this was just the side effects of the pain medication and the trauma of falling again, as she had never really gotten over the first fall. She had remained terrified of falling, so she barely left her house and used a walker even indoors. What we learned while she was in the skilled nursing rehab facility was that she had dementia, and when her nurse told me she seemed surprised we hadn't known.

Once the word dementia was said, several parts of the last few years fell into place. It was clear we had missed the signs, but because we had all been in this process together, we didn't waste time blaming anyone or wallowing in regrets. We just moved on to what it meant, and the recommendation was that she move to memory care. The staff was amazing in helping us find not only an available memory care bed, but one that was close by that came recommended and took Medicaid. I had started the conversation with aging services two years earlier, and with the diagnosis of dementia we knew it was likely she'd qualify for Medicaid. So, five weeks after she fell, with her broken tailbone on the mend, she moved into her new home at the memory care cottage, and we all exhaled.

The last chapter of my mother's story is still being written, but I can say that as I write this, she is stable and thankfully not in any pain. We decided that continuing to push her to rehab was not working, and it was hard on us to spend our effort trying to force her to be compliant. We had heard from several people whose loved ones had been in hospice, that their biggest regret was that they didn't start hospice care sooner. Hospice isn't only for the last few weeks but can offer support to both the patient and the family for months or even years if needed. So, instead of spending our time being coaches and therapists, we now get to spend our time being daughters and grandchildren. We get to just *be* and not *do*. We can also shift our focus to what comes next in our own lives and focus on living. We recently celebrated Mom's 90th birthday with a homemade cake, singing and telling stories. We hope she will be here to meet her new great-grandchild who will arrive in November, but if not then we will be okay. We are secure in our decision, and we are all able to sleep better knowing she is receiving quality care from a loving and compassionate staff, and that when she is gone, we will still be a family.

Marigolds on a Ledge

A Child's Wish

give me a riddle and sing me a song
go on a trip and take me along
draw me a picture with colors so bright
they sparkle and glow when you turn out the light
make ugly faces and stick out your tongue
lift me up high to the ladder's top rung
make me a rocket and see if it flies
win me a goldfish and see if it dies
read me a story with goblins and gnomes
follow the birds til we find all their homes
do something funny and witty and clever
just promise me this: stay with me for ever

A Bench in the City

Ernie's Pond

Tammy Hurst, RN, MSN, NC-BC

Tammy, a Registered Nurse with nearly 30 years of experience, is dedicated to women's health and well-being. Throughout her career, she has specialized in various aspects of women's health, from prenatal care to postpartum support. Tammy's passion for holistic care led her to become a certified Nurse Coach. Tammy's approach is rooted in addressing life challenges holistically, considering the physical, emotional, and spiritual aspects of health. She believes in empowering women to take charge of their own well-being through personalized guidance and support. Her work has been transformative for her clients, helping them achieve greater health, fulfillment, and resilience. Tammy is also a dedicated mother and wife and an advocate for self-care and work-life balance, with a strong belief that in order to achieve this women need to make themselves their priority.

Tammy Hurst, RN, MSN, NC-BC

The Truth from a Bedside Nurse

I've been a nurse for a long time and have experienced compassion fatigue in varying situations.

I love being a nurse. I have been in Labor and Delivery (L & D) for most of my career. I'm in the job of caring for moms, their families, and their babies. I learned early on that compassion fatigue is just part of the job. Over three decades, it has manifested in different ways.

Poor support, challenging patients, and limited resources all contribute to compassion fatigue, which is a big reason nurses leave the bedside. How have I managed to stay for almost 30 years? I'm not really sure. But what I do know is that compassion fatigue has been slowly pulling me away from the work I thought I'd do forever.

I started in wine country in Northern California. Today, toward the end of my bedside nursing, I am working in one of the most dangerous and beautiful cities in California.

I began my acute care career in nursing at a wonderful hospital. To date, it is the best hospital I have ever worked for. That could be because it's where my training in L & D began, so staff supported my fumbling new knowledge. Or it could be because it was a hospital that truly felt patient care was the top priority.

I recall being called off the floor during one of my shifts to watch a video titled "Give the Customer Their Pickle" (or something similar). The core message was clear: even if it wasn't our standard policy to provide extra diapers to new mothers, the hospital encouraged us to accommodate such requests. The goal was to ensure that our patients had a safe and pleasant experience. This approach made working as a nurse there incredibly rewarding and beautiful.

This hospital had a chaplain whose main job was supporting patients. This chaplain, however, would also check on the nurses when there was a bad baby outcome.

We worked as a team, and we were supported in our collective mission to take the best care of our patients.

I remember that whenever the shit hit the fan and our census was high, our adorable and supportive manager, Sandy, would run down the hall with her heels clicking, yelling, "Don't worry! I'm ordering us all pizza!" It was such a relief to hear those magical words because we all knew that on those days, a lunch break was not going to happen, and even finding time to pee would be a challenge.

During these shifts, being understaffed was one factor leading to compassion fatigue, but it was not the primary cause. The population I served at the time lacked resources for prenatal care and support, which increased the likelihood of challenging medical outcomes.

Being understaffed was tough, but we felt like a team. The hospital cared equally about their nurses as they did their patients. And we felt it. And we supported each other.

During my nearly 30-year RN career, I have worked at six different hospital systems throughout Northern California. Whenever I moved, so did my job. It was important to me to contribute to the community I lived in, by helping care for the people of that community.

After working 10 years in Napa, it was hard to leave. In fact, later I would realize it was the only place where I felt that effective and safe patient care had priority over the bottom line.

In my next job, I found myself in a hospital system that was my first introduction to real dysfunction.

Thus began a 12-year stint at a prestigious Magnet hospital in a city where I knew my kids would get a great education. A city where gifts from patients were common, and every new or experienced mom came in having done all the research about all things having a baby. These were the patients that I'd come home and tell my kids, "Mommy made a friend today."

Along with their depth of knowledge, most of these patients were trusting of the nurses, having been thorough in their research of not just pregnancy but also the physicians, nurses, and hospital. Most patients who came to us knew to look for a Magnet hospital because they would expect to receive a higher level of care.

To become a Magnet hospital is no small feat, and every Magnet hospital should be applauded for their commitment and dedication to the process. The Magnet designation is granted by the American

Nurses Credentialing Center and is based on the job satisfaction of the nurses working there, as well as patient satisfaction and patient outcomes. It all starts, though, with happy nurses.

This implies that happy nurses mean happy patients. Magnet status, among other things, means more money. One survey of 1,400 nurses showed that nurse leaders in Magnet hospitals earn 4.8% more than their colleagues in non-Magnet facilities.[1]

There is not a nurse that I know who doesn't want their hospital to have Magnet status. Why wouldn't we want it? Whatever needs to be done to achieve it, directly benefits us.

But is a Magnet hospital better than one that isn't? In some instances, yes. I'd be the first to argue that the care is better. But not necessarily in all ways.

One afternoon at my Magnet status hospital, I had a heated discussion with a long-time OB doctor about our "drop-in patients" on MediCal, California's state-sponsored health insurance. Frustrated by my insistence on providing equal care to these low-income patients, he snapped and said, "If you want to take care of patients without insurance, you should go work in Africa." His dismissive and bigoted attitude shocked me and emphasized the ongoing challenges in advocating for underserved patients.

This is the same hospital where I witnessed a white OB MD at three o'clock in the morning show his frustration to a "drop in patient" because he'd been called in to evaluate her in the middle of the night. I watched as she yelped in fear and pain, then succumbed to what I saw as physical assault.

---

[1] American Nurses Credentialing Center Testimonials, https://www.nursingworld.org/organizational-programs/magnet/about-magnet/why-become-magnet/testimonials/

I cried for her.

I cried for a system that allowed this.

I cried for witnessing it.

I reported it.

Nothing was done.

He still works there.

I was working at the "best" hospital, and it was the worst. After 12 years, even though it was less than 10 minutes from my house, I left. The feelings of defeat were just too much.

Seeing abuse be ignored, feeling the inequity in the treatment of not only patients but staff along with a "the physicians are always right" mentality, led to compassion fatigue winning out over my dedication to help. It wasn't that I didn't want to take care of my patients; I just got to a point where I couldn't do it anymore. I could no longer bear witness to the imbalance.

I wasn't ready to give up L & D, but I had thought that I'd be at my Magnet hospital forever. Unsure of what to do or where to go, I decided to try something completely different.

I took a job at a call center. There, the system worked great!

There were processes in place that allowed nurses the autonomy to help patients in a way I had never experienced before. We triaged them over the phone based on the symptoms they reported, and we were able to treat them (with standing orders based on symptoms) or send them in the right direction to receive care. It seemed like the perfect job to spend the next 20 years of my career.

About six months in, however, something shifted. I did not feel respected by management. Their focus was on how fast we could get through a call. We were given two minutes off the phone for every hour we worked, and everything we did was recorded. Every click. Every call.

I timed it. When one call ended, the next one came 2.5 seconds later. They never stopped. As an Advice Nurse, we were expected to average 12 minutes per call, and we were evaluated every month for what we were doing wrong. It was only then that we were allowed time away from the phone.

In this hospital system, patients were well aware of their options. As a result, handling communications over the phone often made me the target of some harsh and entitled demands. This took a toll. I started to not care for the person on the other end of the line. I only wanted to make sure I met my quota to avoid receiving a poor evaluation. I hated how I felt, and I began crying every day on my way home.

I knew I was done when a patient kept me on the phone for 15 minutes, yelling at me because the only available appointment for her for her jammed middle finger was in three hours. She was demanding one immediately.

My husband would come home to me feeling sad, miserable, angry, and lost most days. I endured this for two and a half years.

The hospital I work for now, the one I went to after working at the call center, makes me feel like I make a difference. These patients are sicker and do not have access to many resources. They are underserved and underrepresented, in a demographic group whose maternal death rate is on the rise.

Those that trust us, trust us fully. They trust what we advise, the medications that are prescribed, and the care they are given. They are grateful to be cared for through their labor and delivery, even when the care they receive is not the best care available.

Not long ago, we had a patient transferred from a psychiatric hospital. The doctor that had been caring for her warned us that she was the most violent person he had ever come across. When she arrived to have her baby, she wouldn't let us take care of her.

The ones who don't trust us make being a nurse hard. The entirety of a 12-hour shift can be wasted negotiating and navigating how to take care of them. There is no alternative. These women are pregnant, and we need to safely deliver their babies.

As a nurse, I am my care. When I don't feel good about what I do, whatever the reason, it's a heavy burden. When the lack of care is the result of someone not allowing me to do my job because they don't trust me, the providers and the system leave me feeling exhausted, disheartened, and frustrated in a deep, deep way.

After nearly 30 years in nursing, I realized something had to change because I was on the brink of burnout. As nurses, we're trained to keep caring for patients no matter how challenging, disrespectful, or heartbreaking the circumstances, even after a patient has passed away.

When my youngest child went off to college, I suddenly had time for myself—time I had never been allowed before. As I started to focus on self-care, I was amazed at the difference it made. I felt like I had more capacity, more energy, and a renewed sense of purpose.

This personal transformation opened my eyes to a new opportunity: becoming a nurse coach. A nurse coach is a registered nurse who uses their education and expertise to support others through life, taking a holistic approach. This role has transformed both who I am and how I care for others. Through nurse coaching, I've learned that self-care and self-awareness elevate not only how you see yourself but also how you see others and the world around you.

Many moms tend to put their children first because it's a societal expectation. However, what most don't realize is that when you put yourself first, everyone around you benefits.

This realization led me to Nurse Coaching. In this role, I help women recognize their value, reach their potential, and live life on their own terms. The best part? It has made me more self-aware, has made me more compassionate, and has elevated my own life. For every woman I've coached, I've found a common thread that unites us all, reminding us of our shared humanity.

A Faucet in Black and White

Peter Dudley, PCC

Peter is an author, executive coach, and writing coach who tries to make the most of every day. He grew up in Connecticut with summers in Las Vegas, got his electrical engineering degree from UC Berkeley, then went on a long and winding career in startups, nonprofits, and big corporations. Once both his kids were grown, he started Gray Bear Coaching LLC and Gray Bear Publications. Peter has published four novels, two poetry collections, and a chapter book, and his short fiction and professional articles have been published in a wide array of journals and anthologies. He is the founder of Gray Bear Coaching LLC and Gray Bear Publications, and he serves on the board of directors of the San Francisco Writers Conference. Read his articles on leadership, balance, and self-development at graybearcoaching.com. Contact him at peter@graybearcoaching.com.

Peter Dudley, PCC

Show up. Try hard. Be nice.

I didn't realize how exhausting being a caring person in a professional helper role could be until I powered through my first week seeing more than 20 clients. By the end of that week, I had nothing left to give. The exhaustion was profound and existential, in a way I had never felt before. I was truly tapped out. This took me by surprise because I've been through some stuff, and I think I'm pretty resilient.

All my life (57 years and counting), I've been a supportive person. In high school, I was always the trusted confidante with the steady shoulder to cry on (sadly, never the boyfriend). As a manager, I'm people-first, having more concern for the humans I lead than for "hitting the numbers." When I coached youth soccer, my players loved playing on my teams even though we rarely got within sight of a championship.

Throughout my career, I've often been called the calming influence in the room. At the writer's conference where I now volunteer and serve on the board of directors, I joke that I'm the golden retriever of the leadership team—eager to help, always smiling, and able to reduce an attendee's stress just with my presence alone.

That is to say, being supportive and caring comes so naturally to me that I don't usually have to work at it.

So, when this week of 20 clients happened (with 24 more on my calendar for the next week), I wasn't prepared for the knockdown I got. Compassion fatigue hit me hard. Still, it wasn't difficult for me to figure out where it was coming from or what to do about it.

I had only been coaching professionally for about a year, and I had just started a new contract with one of the big-scale mental health providers. This company provides therapy and coaching for employees of their corporate clients. Any of the employees at these companies could pick me out of the catalog and schedule a session with me, and I had opened up my calendar to all of them.

In theory, people would come to me because they saw something in my bio that made them think I'd be the right coach for them. In practice, I had no idea what I would face in that first session. It could be a C-Suite executive wanting to talk about organizational changes, a 76-year-old sales executive terrified of retirement, a mid-career worker going through their first layoff, a young professional eager to get into management, or a father of challenging teens who were being especially difficult.

Or as happened several times during that 20-client week, an employee in their mid-20s, with a job they loved, who would tell me they were "feeling lost" due to a "crippling social anxiety" and what might best be described as a kind of ambiguous existential malaise.

By the third such session that week, I was questioning my ability to perceive reality. These 20-somethings were apparently going through a worse midlife crisis than I or any of my Gen X friends ever had. They talked about feeling lost, about lacking motivation for work, about being fearful of any type of social interaction. They told me they had low self-esteem and terrible imposter syndrome.

And yet, all the facts they presented to me during these discussions indicated they were experiencing what I would call a very normal level of self-doubt and insecurity. They were accomplishing their tasks, making presentations, having fun with friends, interacting positively with colleagues and management, and taking steps for professional and personal development. They talked of positive feedback from their bosses and praise from their peers.

I saw this all as very normal and even mostly positive. But somehow in their minds they were riddled with anxiety, drowning in imposter syndrome, and feeling lost in their careers (which, remember, were just a few years along).

I began to feel numb to their perceived problems. I wanted to reach through the computer to shake them and say, "Get a grip! Get over yourself! Grow up!" It was hard not to begin thinking of these young people as privileged, entitled, and completely unaware of what true hardship looked or felt like.

I have been fortunate and privileged in my life, for the most part. I've had some rough patches of my own, but my Gen X "rub some dirt on it and walk it off" attitude has gotten me through them.

I carry a lot of scar tissue because of that, but I've also developed a lot of resilience.

So, as I listened to them, I started to think about some of the *real* hardships I'd witnessed.

There was the four-time cancer survivor who had just been diagnosed with cancer for the fifth time. She was a regular in my writing group, and one day she shared a journal entry that began, "People tell me I am so strong. But I don't feel strong. I feel broken and exhausted." She wrote about how she felt alone and isolated with her cancer whenever anyone told her she was "strong." It made her feel like an imposter because on the outside she seemed strong to others, but on the inside, she was disintegrating—both physically and emotionally. It made her feel like people had no idea how hard it was for her just to make it through a morning. She was in her mid-60s, I believe. I think that was the last time I saw her.

I thought about the vacation to Nepal I took my family on in 2012. As we walked down the sidewalk at the edge of a vibrant, bustling tourist area in Kathmandu, our guide for the day warned us to step around the naked baby lying unattended. There, at our feet, was an infant no more than three or four months old. It looked like it might be dead, but the guide assured us it was merely sleeping. The baby lay without any blanket or clothing of any kind, on the cold, bare cement. Our guide told us not to pay any attention to it and that its mother was likely somewhere nearby but out of sight, "earning survival any way she can." She then said, "That's how it is in Nepal. If you have money, you live. If you don't, you die." As I've gotten older, I see how in many ways that is true right here in the United States as well.

But even having money isn't enough. I thought about my big sister, seven years older than I, who had a stellar career and retired at 53. Just before she retired, she visited the Bay Area, and we took a walk in Muir Woods among the giant redwood trees. She said, "Peter, you've worked in nonprofits and social impact for a long time. I've spent the first half of my life focused on my career and my family. I would love to do something meaningful with the second half of my life, now that I'll be retiring and my kids will be going off to college." I was eager to help her with that, but when she called a few months later, we had a very different conversation. She told me she had just been diagnosed with ALS. She lived only eight more torturous months. She never got a second half of her life, and she never got to fulfill her vision of helping the world in new ways. My 55th birthday was particularly poignant to me because it was the first number she did not get to celebrate for herself.

And then there was the three-year period of suicidal depression my oldest child went through from ages 19 to 22. Transgender youth have a suicide rate that is four times the rate of their peers, and suicide is the third-leading cause of death among 15- to 24-year-olds.[1] My kid was literally talked off a ledge one night by a compassionate police officer. Over those three years, she checked herself into the hospital numerous times when she was feeling so depressed she didn't trust herself to survive the night. She went through a lot of therapy and counseling. One time, she did attempt

---

[1] The Trevor Project, July 18, 2024: https://www.thetrevorproject.org/resources/article/facts-about-lgbtq-youth-suicide/

to take her own life but immediately regretted it, and she managed to get herself to the hospital before it was too late.

As a father who has stood in the behavioral health ward of a hospital, looked into his child's eyes to see nothing there, and thought *we've really lost her this time*, I had a hard time generating much patience or compassion for these young coaching clients I was supposed to be helping.

As the week dragged on, I pretty much faked my way through the last few sessions, relying on my ability to execute even when my heart wasn't in it.

During all this, I was also supporting my partner who was serving as caregiver for her 88-year-old mother living 500 miles away. Although her mother still lived independently at the time, she'd had a fall and broken a hip, so we had a constant fear of another fall and a nonstop anxiousness about whether mom was safe. That meant that when I wasn't supporting my clients, I was supporting my partner in her own difficult and stressful situation.

I imagine the kind of fatigue that the therapists at the cancer nonprofit I used to work at must go through on a daily, weekly, and monthly basis. Or the doctors and nurses who were hailed as heroes for a hot minute during COVID but who now often get treated worse than retail employees and restaurant serving staff. (For the record, retail and restaurant workers should be treated with the dignity and respect every human deserves. It's a social tragedy that often, they are not.) Most, if not all, not only see and treat people in their worst moments, but then they go home to situations where they're caring for family members as well.

And I wonder at the fortitude of people like my formerly suicidal trans daughter, who is now serving as an EMT in a very conservative part of California. She is regularly called upon to help people who would, in different circumstances, insult, oppress, or even physically harm her. The hate and bigotry directed at transgender people is profoundly destructive and harmful. My daughter willingly and eagerly saves the lives of people who would just as likely tell her to kill herself if they knew she is transgender.

If my daughter can do that, and if my nurse friends can return to the hospital day in and day out, then I can surely figure out how to show up for every one of my coaching clients in the way I truly want to. The 20th client of the week deserves as much of my attention, skill, and compassion as the first, no matter what they need help with.

That weekend, I spent time refreshing and refueling. I got outdoors. I exercised. I slept in. I saw a couple of friends. And I role-reversed with my partner, relying on her for support and coaching instead of being the one to supply the support and coaching. By Monday, I had not only gotten myself back to baseline, but I had also come up with several ways to make sure I would get through the next, more grueling week.

I didn't want to simply recover from this new feeling of compassion fatigue just so I could endure the next week, however. I wanted to build new, healthier habits and techniques that could help me avoid compassion fatigue altogether in the future.

Some of these new habits were focused on self-regulation and resiliency:

- **Planning out my week to avoid burnout**
  My work involves more than just time in session with clients. I have many other projects in flight at any given moment, such as my publishing business, writing weekly articles for my blog, working on personal and professional development, networking, and all the other aspects of running a small business as a solo entrepreneur. Normally, I just keep a rolling to-do list and pull those tasks off the list when I have some free time. Looking ahead at my next week with 24 client sessions scheduled, I intentionally planned out all that other, non-client work for the days with fewer meetings. This allowed me to direct my attention to one set of skills more than others on any given day. This is not unlike mixing up workouts at the gym; if you work out several times a week, you don't go all-in on every muscle group every day. You spread it out to work different groups so each group can recover before you hit it hard again.
- **Preparing for and closing out each day**
  On days when I knew I'd have a heavy client load, or clients I knew would be particularly draining, I intentionally steeled myself mentally and emotionally in the morning. This may sound like I created a big, elaborate ritual, but in practice it was just a few minutes of deep, relaxing breaths while reminding myself that I wanted to bring the same caring presence to all my clients. On those days, I would do a similar transition at the end of the day: cleansing

breaths and an intentional letting-go of whatever emotional burdens I had picked up during the day.

- **Using interstitial time for self-management instead of task completion**
  Because I rarely schedule clients back-to-back, I had trained myself to use the 15 or 30 minutes between client calls productively for all those other tasks on my to-do lists. On slower days, this works fine. I can snap into another mode (bookkeeping, customer service, writing, design, networking) for a short time, then transition back into client mode before my session. On busier days, though, I made sure to use that time to get up from my desk, walk around the coworking space or get outside, and perhaps get water or coffee. This small, repeated reset had a remarkably refreshing effect, especially when I left my phone next to my computer.

Other approaches and techniques were aimed at the way I would show up for each session. These keep me in the right frame of mind to give every client my best:

- **Remember that everyone's experience is legitimate**
  One of the things I learned when working at the cancer support nonprofit is that someone else's greater suffering does not invalidate your own, and that someone else's lesser suffering is still suffering. I heard so many cancer patients talk about the guilt they felt because other patients had a worse diagnosis, or worse reactions to chemotherapy, or less

support at home. While it's true that thinking about people who have it worse than you can help you feel gratitude and a different perspective, it's also true that someone else's greater suffering does not invalidate your own. This thought can help build compassion not just for yourself but also for those who have lesser suffering than you. Keeping this in mind helped me remember that just because I or someone I've known has had it worse than my client, that does not invalidate my client's experience. It's not my place to judge what they're living and feeling; it's my job to help them through it. When I feel myself being dragged down into annoyance or apathy for a client, I remind myself of this rule.

- **Remember that each client is engaged in self-improvement**
  These clients came to a coach to help them through a situation they had not yet learned to navigate on their own. Very likely, this was through no fault of their own, especially for the 20-somethings who were raised in an over-scheduled environment, who always received a trophy just for showing up, and who launched into adulthood during lockdown in a global pandemic. Perhaps they should have already had these skills and a better perspective on life, but they didn't. It helps me to think of these clients as actively seeking the tools they were never given, instead of as privileged, entitled, and unaware of what real

hardship looks like. They were coming to me for growth, not to complain.
- **Shift my own goals in the session**
As a coach, my goal in each session is to help my client achieve *their* goal for the session. But sometimes the client is incapable of achieving their goal because they lack the self-awareness to understand what they must do. You can't blame someone for their own lack of experience. A fish, for example, does not know that it is wet. That's because the fish has no concept of *dry*. It only has the experience it has known its whole life, with nothing to compare that to. So it is with many young clients who have very limited life experience. When I found myself beginning to lose patience with a client, this thought would sometimes help. The naïveté of the client was not a willing ignorance, but a lack of perspective. My goal in these cases shifted away from helping them achieve their goal, to helping them see what they needed to learn in order to start working on that goal.
- **Be present "in the now" for myself**
Whenever I feel dragged down, I find refreshment in stepping outside myself to observe what is wonderful about this very moment. A small example of this is when I used to play soccer (before I blew out my knee). If I was getting frustrated with myself for poor performance, I would pause during a break in play and simply focus on taking in the moment. The green grass. The joy of people at play. The broad sky, the fresh air, the birds in the nearby trees, the

light and shadow and motion and sound. Becoming very present in the moment always brought up a feeling of gratitude, which would then lead to peace. This wouldn't necessarily make me perform better on the soccer field, but it always improved my mood. Bringing this technique into my client sessions would similarly lift me up, even when I was on a video call in a tiny "phone booth" style soundproofed room in a coworking space. Just connecting to the physical environment around me was enough to pull me out of my own emotional doldrums.

Most important of all, I keep a picture on my phone of a tee shirt I used to have. It got so threadbare that I decided to retire the shirt and memorialize it in a photo. I don't really need the photo to remember what the shirt said and to have those words remind me of how I want to be. It said:

"Show up. Try hard. Be nice."

That was the motto of my son's high school track team, and really, life does not need to be much more than that. No matter what I feel with any given client at any given moment, I can always show up, try hard, and be nice.

Rainbow Umbrella

Jill Louise Léger

Jill Louise Léger is passionate about the welfare of older adults. She is a credentialed geriatric recreational therapist with over 25 years' experience working and volunteering in long-term care and retirement homes. In 2015, she created The Sunflower Channel, a YouTube hub for short, original videos, each calibrated to meet seniors' physical, intellectual, emotional, social, and spiritual needs both at home and in care facilities. In a past life, Jill was a television producer and researcher, having earned her master's degree in journalism from New York University. An Emmy-nominated researcher, she associate-produced a series for C-SPAN that won a Peabody Award. She served as Head Research Consultant for National Geographic Kids from 2002 to 2008. Follow her Substack, "Bumpy Night," at jill416.substack.com.

Jill Louise Léger

Recreation Therapy & Me: Compassion Fatigue In Elder Care

I was just entering middle age when I switched careers to become a recreation therapist for seniors. Something of a tender-heart, I wondered if daily work in the trenches of long-term care would make me a sitting duck for compassion fatigue. But I was fortunate. Recreation therapy helped me focus on the positive aspects of aging and armed me with tools for enhancing the well-being of those in my care, factors that helped protect me from the grind of compassion fatigue. Even better, it turns out anyone can harness the power of recreation therapy, a highly modifiable discipline that can be applied to any number of caregiving situations.

The year was 2008, and I had just married a Canadian and moved to Toronto from Washington, D.C. The timing was unfortunate. In the wake of the global economic crisis, all the full-time positions in my field (TV production) seemed to have dried up overnight.

Within a year, I found myself at a professional crossroads: keep pursuing short-term contracted work, or find a more stable career.

By then, I'd spent nearly two decades volunteering at long-term-care facilities, retirement homes, and senior day programs. I loved the feeling of brightening a senior's day with a concert or a fun card game. And so many of the older adults I met had incredible stories to tell—surviving the London Blitz, jitterbugging at the Apollo in Harlem, marching with Martin Luther King Jr. My first volunteer gig was at a small nursing home in Greenwich Village, where I passed out napkins and refreshments as a showman named Curvie McMurray brought down the house with his sing-along versions of jazzy standards. Later, in D.C., I volunteered at a home on Thomas Circle, where I created a weekly activity night featuring games, trivia, poetry, and karaoke. I'd stock up on sugar-free cookies from the CVS across the street, flick on my microphone, and away we'd go. In Toronto, I began participating in a weekly music night at a high-end retirement home in the West End. Curious about a career working with seniors, I asked an employee there how she got her job, and she told me about a geriatric recreational-therapy program at a local college—a two-year course of study that churned out recreation therapists as fast as the city's growing number of senior-living facilities could hire them.

Two and a half years later, I was one of those fresh graduates, a newly minted recreation therapist about to discover that daily work in a nursing home is much different than fluttering in once a week like a butterfly with a karaoke machine and a package of cookies. I soon found myself in a run-down facility with a creaky elevator, a leaky ceiling, and a not-so-small ant problem. Physically, the job was rough, requiring the regular lifting of cumbersome activity tables and finagling of heavy wheelchairs into tight spaces. And emotionally, it was a minefield, rife with sickness, suffering, decline, and, as I would learn all too well, death.

But my work helped me keep an upbeat mindset. Recreation therapists are trained to look for the positive, determining what a person is still able to do and identifying the optimal methods of meeting his or her needs through meaningful activities and personalized interventions. These can run a very wide gamut. You're probably familiar with the typical activities associated with nursing homes—bingo, singalongs, therapy-pet visits, and so forth. But at a good facility, there's usually a lot more going on. Maybe a war veteran is being interviewed for an oral history project or a podcast. Maybe a knitter is making a blanket for a charity organization, or an avid reader is enjoying a book checked out from the local library. If so, you can almost certainly thank a recreation therapist.

Recreation therapy can be powerful, and in senior populations it is clinically proven to ease depression, increase socialization, and enhance feelings of self-worth. It wasn't long before I began to see for myself evidence that my work was making a positive difference—both in my own documentation and in the smiles on residents' faces. Such affirmation was enough to keep me going, even on the most challenging days. (Until it wasn't, but that's a story for later in this chapter.)

In school, I'd learned that recreation therapy is all about the unmet need. Older adults, especially those living in assisted care, typically have a lot of these due to changes in life circumstances. Imagine living without companionship, exercise, intellectual stimulation, validation, purpose, and independence, and then consider that this is the situation many elders face, day after day, year after year. Seniors' basic needs are typically divided into five general categories: physical, intellectual, emotional, social, and spiritual. Any meaningful activity, intervention, or interaction will target at least one of these and usually a combination. Sometimes, needs are obvious. An ardent gardener, for example, might have an emotional need to be outdoors with her hands in the dirt, or a devout Catholic might have a spiritual need to attend a weekly religious service. But sometimes identifying needs can require a little sleuthing. This process can involve everything from consulting an initial assessment to talking to family members to chatting up the resident themselves, all to get a sense of that person's background, hobbies, religion, interests, and so on. Every tidbit of information can be an important clue to determining the most meaningful and effective ways of applying recreation therapy.

I discovered early on that careful detective work can reap big dividends.

Take Mrs. R., who was notoriously cranky. Always elegantly turned out in full makeup and jewelry, she was a serial complainer for whom even the smallest disappointments were outright "travesties." Examples that spring to mind include not enough pepper in her pepper shaker, no marigolds at the botanical garden we visited, my "inadequate" description of the physics behind time-travel theory, the sensory assault that was my fanny pack, "cheap" maple syrup at a pancake breakfast, and me calling too many Bs in a row during bingo. This joyless woman was an utter mystery to me until I had a moment one day to check her initial assessment, whereupon I discovered that she had once expressed a love of poetry. The next day, I stopped by her room with a couple books I'd checked out at the library the previous evening. After knocking on her open door, I said hello and casually asked if she happened to like poetry. She was in her wheelchair, between the bed and the window, peering at herself despairingly in a round compact mirror as she feverishly patted at her face with a powder puff. She turned her head and glared at me, her annoyance melting away as my question sank in.

"Poetry?" she said, eyeing the books in my hand.

She took the first one and paged through it, stopping at a poem by Phyllis McGinley.

"Oh!" she sighed with a small smile, her eyes taking in the page.

"Want me to read it to you?" I asked.

"Oh, yes," she said. She settled a bit into her chair and folded her hands before looking at me expectantly.

The poem was called "The 5:32," a little jewel of a piece about a woman picking up her husband every day at a train station. As I read, I felt my heart expanding to its simple humanity, thinking sentimentally of my own husband. At one point, my voice actually cracked, but Mrs. R. didn't appear to notice. She was caught up in her own thoughts, and when the poem concluded, I noticed that her eyes were watery.

And that was how I reached Mrs. R. We read poems regularly after that, stealing moments together to share our favorites or immerse ourselves in new ones. Oftentimes, some image or turn of phrase would get Mrs. R. talking about her past, usually a memory that seemed to bring her pleasure. Admittedly, Mrs. R. didn't change overnight; she remained an essentially crabby and demanding person. But there was no doubt she was smiling more and seemed better able to access an inner reserve of patience. She was even more chill about repeated Bs in bingo.

And then there was Mr. K., a septuagenarian who'd been in a car accident a decade earlier that had left him unable to walk. Though he could be persuaded to participate in all manner of activities, his default mode struck me as self-pitying. When asked how he was doing, Mr. K. often replied with a sullen "thumbs down" gesture as he rolled through the hallway. I knew from his robust participation in every singalong that he loved music, but it wasn't until I dug around a little that I learned he also enjoyed *writing* songs. When I asked him about this one afternoon, he immediately began to sing an infectious little tune about falling in love with a shy farmgirl. As he crooned, I had an idea. We had a holiday party coming up, replete with a "floor show" featuring the home's bell choir and a roster of guests singing carols and other holiday numbers. What if we could transcribe Mr. K.'s song and create a piano arrangement? And what if he could take part in the show and sing his song for all the attendees? I recorded him singing the tune and was able to create a first pass of sheet music. I sent my work to a friend, who kindly used it to create a sound file, a backing track that Mr. K. could use during the performance. Mr. K. and I practiced his song together, and I recruited another resident to play the part of "shy farmgirl" so he'd have someone to serenade.

Mr. K. never looked snazzier than the afternoon he wheeled into the party. Maybe it was his smile, his blue necktie, or the pride he exuded. And naturally, his song was a hit, and he was treated like a rock star for the rest of the event as people showered him with compliments and (in at least one instance) autograph requests. After that, Mr. K.'s demeanor improved noticeably, and I can recall documenting about three weeks later that his "thumbs down" gesture had all but vanished.

A third example may be even more to the point. One new resident experiencing dementia was always asking for a can of beer, becoming agitated when his request was denied. One of my colleagues called his wife and determined his favorite brand. On her next shift, she brought in an empty can, which she gave to the nursing staff on his floor. The next time the resident asked for a beer, the nurses gave him the can filled with water. The tactic worked like a charm, because it turned out all he really needed was the emotional comfort of his routine.

It was small triumphs like these that kept me going. The job was tough, but I was buoyed by the creative challenge of figuring out how to add magic and light to the lives of those residents. I dutifully awoke before dawn to work the griddle at the home's monthly pancake breakfast, created an art display of residents' takes on Van Gogh's sunflowers, produced and edited a monthly video newsletter, helped stage an elaborate Winter Olympics opening ceremony replete with a flame made of tissue paper and the stiff tube at the center of a roll of plastic wrap… anything and everything I could think of. I felt unstoppable.

That it was a sad and run-down place only fueled my fire, as if I were trying to compensate for its shortcomings. Part of a tiny recreation staff of three supporting just over 100 residents, I think we all felt that way. Assisted-care homes are complex, interconnected places, where any deficiency—be it understaffing or a building that's physically deteriorating—can result in systemic dysfunction, which residents can and do pick up on.

I sometimes found it absurd how much we did to try to make up for the overall decrepitude around us. We pulled off more than two dozen programs a week (way more than comparable homes executed). We planned parties and outings, hired talent, ordered clothing, and decked the halls for every conceivable holiday. And, because there was no one else to do it, we troubleshot. Our small office was directly across the hall from the elevator, making it a natural first stop for anyone in need. One couple was always losing their TV signal and routinely desperate for someone to come upstairs and fiddle with their cable box. I used up an entire tube of Shoe Goo repairing the perpetually loose sole of one guy's ancient loafer. At least once a week, Mrs. L. would roll up with a bottle of blue or green nail polish requesting an urgent manicure. And one elegant and lucid woman would park herself in our office every day to tell us she was sick of the indignity of living there and just wanted to die. We coped with TVs and DVD players that never worked, eternally rotten phone reception, wobbly armchairs, wonky plumbing. We cared for the home's messy budgies, cleaned out and organized dozens of boxes jam-packed with holiday decorations (one containing a very rotten pumpkin), called the police when residents went missing, and, on an evening I'll never forget, fended off a resident's "boyfriend" who turned up at the front door, restraining order be damned. Punctuating all these scenes was the mournful moan of Mr. M. on the second floor, a primal howl erupting every ten minutes or so, resonating up to the third floor and down to the first, reminding us all that we weren't in Kansas anymore.

But I believed this was where I needed to be, where I could make the most difference. Not some fancy over-funded retirement home with a baby grand piano in the lobby. I'm not exactly what you would call a religious person, but a part of me believed I was doing God's work.

And then everything went to hell.

I'd been at that home about a year and a half when my direct supervisor resigned, followed not long afterwards by the only other recreation therapist. As if that weren't disruptive enough, the kindly administrator who'd hired me got reassigned to another facility, and another woman took her place. That's when I discovered that there was one thing I couldn't tolerate as a recreation therapist, and that was a lack of managerial support.

I should have been suspicious when she showed up in heels.

Not long after the new administrator started, she let it be known that she would be requiring photographic proof of every activity. I cynically believed this had something to do with funding, or maybe so she could assure residents' family members that their relatives were leading their best lives under her leadership. Whatever the case, it was a command that was very disruptive to our work. Instead of focusing on a given program or intervention, we now needed to pull away and take pictures. And because we had no departmental smart phones back then, we had to use a digital camera that had seen better days, then upload and label the photos before moving them to a central folder. This was a tedious and time-consuming process, given our painfully slow computer.

The new administrator seldom responded to emails and was prone to making and then casually forgetting important promises and deadlines, which meant we could be waiting weeks for, say, a new department budget to be approved. Already outspoken, I pissed her off one day when I reacted poorly to her interrupting my conversation with the new recreation manager. ("Excuse me," I'd said somewhat recklessly. "I was talking to Julie.") All hell broke loose after that. Later that day, while I was upstairs with a resident, I heard the administrator's voice repeatedly paging me to come down to the front office. When I showed up, she calmly informed me from behind her desk that I was being suspended for insubordination and needed to pack up my things and go home for the rest of the week. Burning with anger and shock, I sobbed all the way home in a cab ("please don't do anything to harm yourself," the gentle cabbie said as he pulled up to my house) and over the weekend decided it was time to resign.

The next home promised to be much better. Their terrific recreation manager and administrator seemed to appreciate my skills, and every day I found myself surrounded by friendly staff and residents. And then, wouldn't you know it, the same thing happened. Within a year, both my manager and the administrator quit. The two spots remained vacant for weeks, but clearly someone was in charge, because strange things started happening. One day, we watched maintenance clear out our little recreation office, which within days was co-opted by higher-ranking staff. I arrived one morning to find our computer moved near the corner of the main recreation room, which meant we were often forced to do our documentation during a noisy activity or meeting. Then signs went up in the same room saying that recreation staff could no longer stash coats and purses in certain closets and were instead to stuff belongings into a pair of designated cabinet drawers. It became mandatory that each therapist assist with feeding a higher-needs resident at all mealtimes. Then we were suddenly saddled with the job of watering all the outdoor shrubs, plants, and flowers—an inconvenient task to say the least. The row of bushes along the back side of the home was so far from the hose that you needed to cart a bucket of water across the lawn, watering three or four plants at a time before having to go back to the spigot. And then, alas, this place too began placing a strong emphasis on getting lots of photos to prove that an activity took place or was well-attended. I remember watching in dismay as one of my fellow rec therapists woke a woman sound asleep in her bed so that she and a few other staff could sing to her on her 100th birthday, regale her with flowers and balloons, and of course, take lots of pictures.

When a department colleague was fired allegedly for wearing capri pants too many days in a row, my morale sank even lower.

And then COVID happened, which ended up breaking me for good, not because I didn't want to risk my health on the front lines, but because I didn't trust the home's new management to protect me. It seemed to me they were more interested in preserving the recreation department's status quo (what I thought of as "ticking boxes") than they were in making useful changes and adjustments. More than once, I felt forced to enter dangerous environments unnecessarily, which I found infuriating. This same inflexibility seemed to apply to how the home cared for the residents as well. There was one floor where every day, I saw residents lined up in their wheelchairs, one after the other up and down a fluorescently lit hallway. Because they could no longer leave the floor, this is where they remained from breakfast to bedtime, their days broken up only by meals, snacks, and visits from us. This lasted for months. We did our best to make their lives bearable, playing music and videos, leading games, facilitating Zoom calls, but we couldn't be there all the time. I regarded the lack of natural light and the perpetual sameness as horrific, and I could see these residents declining before my eyes. I had never felt so powerless, running into opposition whenever I asked if they could be moved to the window or that their spots be varied throughout the day. When the facility experienced literally the largest long-term-care COVID outbreak in the province of Ontario, I decided that enough was enough. After six months on the front lines, I resigned and took an office job. I've never looked back.

So I guess you could say that compassion fatigue got me in the end, manifested by institutional deficiencies that made me feel unsupported and powerless as I tried to cope with already-fraught caregiving situations. It was my sad experience to discover that nothing saps energy and enthusiasm quite like being forced to deal with the wrong employees in the wrong positions. But I hasten to add that I met so many terrific people while working in long-term care. Three fellow employees remain good friends, and many more I continue to see at least a couple times a year. Overall, my experience was a positive one, and I feel good about the work I did and the people I tried to help. It's even possible that one day I will return to the profession. I loved the fact that it grounded me in what is real and forced me to be in the moment every day, my focus far removed from my own ego. Perhaps one day I might even go freelance and offer my skills to caregivers looking for assistance.

The good news is that you don't need an institutional environment to make recreation therapy work for you. It can be practiced anywhere and applied to virtually any caregiving situation. A description of how it works is included at the end of this chapter. I believe that once you have a sense of these fundamentals, the rest will be easy. Here are some basic tips to get you started.

Start Simple

The simplest interventions can often address all kinds of needs and offer great therapeutic benefits. Examples might include facilitating a regular phone call with a friend or leading a few seated exercises set to upbeat music. One often-overlooked need is also one of the easiest to address: sensory stimulation. Sensory deprivation alone—lack of sunlight, human touch, and sensory variations such as new sights, smells, tastes, sensations, and sounds—can be extraordinarily detrimental to a person's well-being, leading to depression and decline all by itself. Addressing it can be as easy as loading up a tray with a few herbs and letting a care recipient smell or taste each sprig, or plugging in a string of twinkle lights and playing soft jazz. I remember one woman who expressed a feeling of peace whenever she watched her "rainbow maker," a solar-powered crystal that slowly rotated in her window, refracting sunlight to create spectrums of color that danced along the walls.

Celebrate the Now

My mother was a fan of the 1940s-era song "Ac-Cent-Tchu-Ate the Positive," which happens to be a perfect mantra for recreation therapy. The aim is to seek out the positive and then validate, celebrate, and help perpetuate all the things a person can still do. Help a care recipient continue to exercise, stay connected with others, and pursue past interests even if his or her abilities to do so are changing. And bonus points if you can find a way for a care recipient to help *you*. For example, if an older relative can still remember how to tell when a turkey is done, or which day of the year taxes are due, or the principles behind driving a stick shift, or who starred in *Now, Voyager*, by all means, ask her! Utilize every bit of expertise she has, because not only will she almost certainly feel valued and validated, her answer could very well turn out to be helpful.

Be Observant and Stay Nimble

Some care recipients, such as frail seniors, can be highly sensitive to their environments, responding to the unspoken moods of others and to sometimes-subtle room conditions such as lighting, temperature, and background noise. If someone is unresponsive, or, worse, is acting out for no apparent reason, become a detective and consider what might be triggering such a behavior. (It will always come down to an unmet physical or psychosocial need.) You might discover a cause that can be addressed in the moment, such as giving the person a sweater or closing the blinds.

But if you come up short, don't worry. Try switching things up with a new location or another time of day. Often, small variations can do the trick in ways that might surprise you. For example, I'd always played classical music during a seated "gentle stretch" program until one day, I noticed my group looking bored and distracted. I spontaneously popped in a Huey Lewis CD that was lying around, and *voila!* My seniors began rocking out to "Power of Love," singing and smiling as they reached their hands up to the ceiling.

Online and Community Resources for Recreation Therapy

Once you start searching, you might be surprised to discover the wealth of online resources dedicated solely to keeping certain demographics challenged, entertained, and busy. For example, there are dozens if not hundreds of websites devoted to senior-geared games, quizzes, jokes, puzzles, and activity ideas. And be sure to check out YouTube, where you'll find recreation therapy videos catering to all kinds of levels and interests.

One channel especially close to my heart is called The Sunflower Channel[1], which I created in 2015 especially for caregivers of older adults wanting to bring recreation therapy into their homes. There you will find dozens of videos, each one designed to meet one or more of the five primary needs. They span a wide gamut, from sensory stimulation, seated exercise and yoga to singalongs, conversation starters, seated tap-dancing, and more. In the information section of each video is a description of the therapeutic benefits and the specific needs being targeted.

There are also lots of community organizations you can lean on. For seniors living alone, I'm a particular fan of phone-based programs designed to engage older adults via friendly conversations, group discussions, and even classes. And most communities have "day programs" for the elderly, where trained staff run therapeutic activities, typically from morning to mid-afternoon. Many cater to a wide variety of needs and can provide door-to-door transportation, as well as a home-made lunch.

Outsource!

As I hinted at earlier, many credentialed recreation therapists (RTs) choose to go freelance, creating their own client lists and schedules. An RT will come to a private home or facility, meet with you and your relative, and conduct a careful assessment. The RT will then create an individualized care plan that can focus on any area

---

1 The Sunflower Channel: https://www.youtube.com/@thesunflowerchannel5361

of concern, such as depression, irritability, responsive behaviors, restlessness, and so on. Together, you and the RT can determine a schedule most conducive to the needs of both you and the care recipient. Then, while you're catching up on errands or "me time," an RT can be taking your relative to lunch or a movie, challenging him or her to a game of Scrabble, or just wiling away an hour or two conversing on a park bench. (Never underestimate the power of simple time and curiosity. You've probably heard your relative's stories a thousand times, but an RT comes to them fresh and open, which can amp up the therapeutic benefits a senior might reap simply from having a chance to share.) RTs typically charge by the hour and can have an extraordinary effect on the well-being of a frail or isolated senior.

Recreation Therapy Works!

When I'm explaining the positive effects of recreation therapy, I usually present as evidence a viral video from a few years back of an older, frail adult donning a pair of headphones and hearing a favorite song. His face erupts into an expression of such profound engagement and delight, you can practically see the serotonin and dopamine firing away in his brain.

I saw these kinds of reactions countless times. Maybe it was when we surprised Mr. L. with a family Zoom call during the pandemic, or when a grade-school class showed up to sing "You Are My Sunshine" at the foot of Mrs. T.'s bed, or when we pulled off an especially rousing party where even the most desolate soul was clapping along and singing. On those occasions, the discipline of recreation therapy seemed to soar into a higher realm, and all at once, these vulnerable, vibrant humans seemed to be connecting not only with others but also with their best and truest selves. Something wonderful filled the air. And if the residents were feeling something akin to joy, perhaps just as important, so was I.

Sunflower with Blue Sky

Rereation Therapy 101

How Does Recreation Therapy Work?

Recreation therapy can help mitigate compassion fatigue by empowering caregivers with tools and tricks for enhancing the lives of care recipients. Clinically proven to ease depression and increase socialization in older adults, rec therapy is designed to slow decline and enhance well-being by targeting unmet needs.

In senior populations, basic needs fall into five general categories: physical, intellectual, emotional, social, and spiritual. A trained recreation therapist can identify an individual's unmet needs and then determine a whole host of meaningful, person-centered ways to meet them. Unmet needs (especially in elderly populations) can not only hasten decline; they can also trigger what are known as "responsive behaviors," unwanted and sometimes disruptive and violent behaviors such as verbal and physical abuse.

What is a "Meaningful" Activity?

In a senior-living facility, the nuts and bolts of a good recreation department are its group activities, which are explicitly designed to meet one or more of the five primary needs. A seated exercise program, for example, can promote physical as well as emotional and social well-being. A yoga program might strive to meet not only emotional, physical, and social needs, but spiritual needs as well. A simple sensory-based activity during which a bedridden resident is given herbs to smell and a hand massage with lavender-scented lotion can address the need for social contact and, vitally, the emotional need for different kinds of sensory experiences. One-on-one music therapy—tonal bell-ringing, for example—might promote intellectual well-being along with the emotional satisfaction of hearing, and being able to play, a familiar song. A "reminiscing roundtable," in which residents share memories specific to a time period, photograph, or event, can make participants feel socially connected with their peers and emotionally validated through the acts of sharing and listening. Such a program can also help meet intellectual needs by challenging residents to remember the past and articulate it in a way that might be interesting to their peers.

Each activity must meet a set of specified therapeutic goals, outlined in a document called an *activity plan*. For example, a seated exercise program might be designed to provide participants with the following benefits:

- To attain and maintain fullest physical potential.
- To prevent physical deterioration and decline.
- To maintain or improve range of motion, circulation, and muscle tone.
- To enhance social and emotional well-being by fostering a spirit of shared fun with fellow residents.
- To provide sensory stimulation and promote emotional well-being through music.

An activity plan should also specify quantifiable objectives that will determine if these goals are being met and therefore if the program is successful. Additionally, it must indicate staffing requirements, optimal group size, and any necessary equipment and/or supplies. Once all this has been incorporated, the activity can be taken out for a spin to see how well it works.

Initial Assessments and Care Plans

But which residents stand to benefit the most from a given program? Matching individuals to programs can be trickier than you might think and requires a thoughtful understanding of every single person living in the facility. Or as they say in showbiz, "you gotta know your audience."

Knowing your residents begins with an *initial assessment*. For the recreation department, this process usually involves an interview with the new arrival to find out about his or her background, hobbies, family, recreation preferences, and so on. Each answer then gives shape to a recreation *care plan*, which will delineate all the ways the department can help meet the new arrival's needs and thus promote a sense of well-being.

A care plan will usually begin with a list of all the recreation programs determined to be most appropriate for the resident—Knitting Circle for an avid knitter, pet-therapy visits for an animal lover, and so forth. The care plan might instruct the department to practice cultural sensitivities, such as greeting a person in his or her first language or making sure to observe days of the year that might be important to the resident such as Rosh Hashana, Robbie Burns Day, or Chinese New Year. And it will almost always suggest personalized, therapeutic interventions such as providing an avid reader with a department Kindle, making sure a bedside radio is always set to a person's favorite station, or ensuring that people of the same cultural background are seated together at mealtimes.

A care plan will also include a set of "big picture" goals, each one articulating what all these activities and interventions when taken together will optimally achieve for the resident. This list often starts with basic, "evergreen" goals, such as "maximize Mrs. C.'s well-being," "foster Mrs. C.'s independence," "minimize Mrs. C.'s decline," and so on. Over time, this list will usually evolve and grow as the department learns more about a resident's specific personality and needs. As with activity plans, goals are always accompanied by sets of quantifiable objectives so that the department can discern whether they are being met.

Each new resident's recreation care plan is stored in a centralized database, where it can be accessed by any employee. Because each department (dietary, nursing, and physiotherapy, for example) is also sharing its own care plan, the person's new home stands a decent chance of aligning with individual preferences and needs across all aspects of care, smoothing the new resident's assimilation.

Case Study #1: Mrs. C.

A new resident, Mrs. C., is a gardener, a bookworm, a devout Catholic, and an animal-lover. She has her own iPad, seems very sociable, likes singing and board games, and isn't opposed to a little mild exercise. And, she once told you she loves dancing and used to attend the ballet.

1. Invite Mrs. C. to an orientation "Tea & Talk" and encourage conversation with her fellow residents.
2. Invite Mrs. C. to Gardening Group, Reading Circle, Book Club, Library Visits, Catholic Mass, Trivia Tuesday, Cards & Crosswords, Bingo, Sunshine Singalong, Seated Exercise, Seated Yoga, and all parties and performances in the main dining room.
3. Schedule Mrs. C. for weekly therapy-dog visits.
4. Schedule Mrs. C. for weekly blessings from the visiting Catholic priest.
5. Create a customized iPad playlist of music and podcasts Mrs. C. might enjoy.
6. Help Mrs. C. find and download games and other kinds of apps she might enjoy on her iPad.
7. Create a one-time "History of Dance" program, incorporating some of Mrs. C.'s favorite steps and choreographers. Invite interested residents and encourage Mrs. C.'s socialization.
8. Investigate the possibility of using department funds to purchase Mrs. C. and her daughter tickets to the ballet or other local dance performance.

Admittedly, Mrs. C. was pretty easy. She was already the kind of person who openly engaged with her world, and the odds were therefore favorable that she might benefit from the kinds of programs and interventions the home could offer. But most new residents are more challenging.

Case Study #2: Mr. J.

Mr. J. has mild dementia, tells you he's never been a "joiner," and prefers to be left alone in his room. He says he has no interest in any of the programs currently in place, not even "self-administered" activities such as listening to music in his room, reading the daily newspaper, or playing Solitaire. This is where you might need to dig a little deeper, looking for any information that can shed light on what makes him tick. After speaking with Mr. J.'s daughter, you learn that Mr. J. served in the Army, is very close to his daughter and granddaughter, likes watching baseball on TV, and worked for decades as a plumber. With just these bits of information, you could be off to the races. Here are some ideas I might include in Mr. J.'s recreation care plan, each one designed to make him feel validated, ease his assimilation into the home, and foster a sense of identity and purpose.

1. Ask the family for permission to display copies of photos from Mr. J.'s days in the armed forces. Encourage staff to thank Mr. J. for his service and engage him in relevant conversation.
2. Include Mr. J. in Remembrance Day programs and be sure that he is always honored by name.
3. Encourage Mr. J. to share memories of his time in the service. This can take place in small group settings (reminiscence programs), in one-on-one discussions, and/or as part of our home's Oral History Project.

4. Encourage, schedule, and facilitate regular visits between Mr. J. and his daughter and granddaughter, either in person or via Zoom.
5. Invite Mr. J. to all parties and performances in the main dining room and encourage socialization. Invite Mr. J.'s daughter and granddaughter to these events to help encourage his attendance and enhance his comfort level.
6. Engage the maintenance department to ask for Mr. J.'s input on one real-world, plumbing-related issue at least once a month.
7. Engage Mr. J.'s help sorting mechanical pieces like nuts and bolts for the maintenance department. (Sorting activities can often be a great task for people with dementia.)
8. Invite Mr. J. as a "special guest" to Men's Group Roundtable to share his career and experiences with other residents. If he participates, be sure to encourage him join the group again.
9. Be sure Mr. J.'s cable plan allows him to watch major-league baseball games in his room. Within his first three months, introduce him to other baseball fans on his floor, such as Mr. R. and Mrs. P. If he is amenable to it, help facilitate a small group of fans to watch a game together in his room or in the common room on his floor.
10. Investigate a group trip to see a Blue Jays game with Mr. J. and other residents.

The idea is to find ways to help meet Mr. J.'s needs while still honoring his overall preference to be left alone. This care plan is just a starting point. Over time, depending on how well these interventions work, the plan may change. And even if a suggestion flops, Mr. J. can still benefit from our having tried. A cardinal rule of senior care is giving a person agency and choice at every opportunity. The very act of inviting someone to do something is showing that person respect and providing them with an opportunity to exercise the power of choice. A "no" might not be the answer you want, but the fact that a resident has made and expressed this choice, and that you are accepting it, can be therapeutic in itself.

Determining Success

To learn if a given activity is working, a recreation therapist must first establish the quantitative measures that will determine whether the activity's stated goals are being met. A seated exercise program, for example, might be considered successful if at least 80% of the participants are either following or attempting to follow each exercise move. Or a singalong activity might be deemed successful if at least 85% of the participants are either singing, clapping, or tapping their toes to each song. Each program is always evaluated after it takes place, and if it falls short, adjustments are made until it works.

Quantifiable objectives will also help determine if the recreation department is meeting the "big picture" goals delineated in a resident's care plan. A goal like "maximize Mrs. C.'s well-being" means nothing if the care plan doesn't also specify how this somewhat nebulous outcome can be measured. Here are some examples of quantifiable objectives that could serve as evidence of Mrs. C.'s overall "well-being" (once staff has had a chance to get to know her individual needs and personality profile):

- Mrs. C. will attend at least five recreation activities each week.
- Mrs. C.'s responsive behaviors will be reduced by 50% as compared with the previous three-month period.
- Mrs. C. will give a positive answer to "How are you?" at least 75% of the time.
- Mrs. C. will actively engage with her tablemates at least once during each lunchtime period.

The degree to which these "big picture" goals are met sheds light on how well an overall care plan is working, and, by extension, how well the recreation staff is working to address a resident's needs. And once a goal is met, the department might choose to keep it, tweak it, or replace it. Care plans are always changing—just like care recipients themselves.

Special Cases: The Very Frail

Individuals who are extremely ill or are experiencing advanced dementia can present special challenges. Maybe they spend most of their time in bed or have trouble sharing things about themselves in the first place. In such cases, I suggest beginning with a simple one-on-one visit to find out what you can, and later, if necessary, track down family members and friends to learn more about their life story and personal preferences. Keep in mind that many people experiencing even later-stage dementia can still recall details of their childhoods and might be eager to share stories about that time. Such conversations can unexpectedly reveal other interests and preferences, helping you connect that resident to suitable activities and interventions, or even to other residents.

I also suggest trying to build one-on-one activities around, say, favorite films, perfumes, flowers, colors, food, poems, artists, and so on. Sorting activities too can be fun and challenging and are highly therapeutic. These might include organizing a cluster of paperclips by color or matching up socks from a "laundry" pile.

For individuals in the very advanced stages of ill health or dementia, sensory-based programs incorporating hand massage, soft music, aromatherapy, or the like can be highly beneficial, addressing emotional, social, physical, and even spiritual needs all in one go.

When interacting with people experiencing dementia, always try to engage in their reality, especially if they are feeling anxious or agitated. Emotionally, an upset elder needs comfort and reassurance, not frustration and more agitation, which is a common reaction when a "well-meaning" person is dismissive or contradictory. So, if an octogenarian tells you she just had a baby, congratulate her and ask if it was a boy or a girl!

Creeping Chameleon

Dr. Kenya Oscar Radoli

Dr. Kenya Oscar Radoli, founder of KOR Navigation Consulting and Coaching, is a visionary leader with over two decades of experience in business innovation and digital transformation. He manages multimillion-dollar projects, nurtures talent, and fosters diverse, innovative cultures. His leadership consistently elevates project and portfolio management standards, bridging gaps between diverse constituencies and exceeding expectations. Throughout his career, Dr. Radoli has turned ideas into action, seized opportunities, and designed innovative solutions that enhance operations, talent, revenues, and profits. His passion for developing high-performing leaders and staff on complex projects has driven his success. Dr. Radoli's international experience positions him as a strategic partner for C-suite leaders seeking to develop inclusive organizational cultures and public-private partnerships (PPPs) in the U.S. and Africa. He sits on the University of Pennsylvania Nonprofit Leadership Alumni Board. He holds degrees from Clarion University of Pennsylvania, University of Pennsylvania, and a Doctorate from the University of Pittsburgh.

Dr. Kenya Oscar Radoli

Nurturing Resilience: Practical Strategies for Organization Change Leaders

As a Diversity, Equity, and Inclusion (DEI) practitioner, I play a crucial role in architecting and fostering inclusive environments to drive positive change within organizations. The nature of this work often exposes me to emotional labor and vicarious trauma, leading to burnout. Some of the common challenges I face working to improve organizational cultures are

- A lack of DEI understanding
- Organization Inertia
- A lack of support
- Opposition
- Emotional toll

These difficulties are not limited to the DEI space. They affect many roles within organizations. Through my career, my education, and my experience playing and coaching international rugby, I have developed traits and skills that have built my resilience to the compassion fatigue that can result from prolonged work in this type of situation.

Understanding the Landscape

Working in the innovation space, I am inspired by something Steve Jobs said: "Innovation is the ability to see change as an opportunity—not a threat." This quote can be applied to anyone driving change in their organization. Resistance to change is a natural human instinct, but it's often magnified by a failure to understand the benefits of moving forward. Without comprehension, there can be no consent, so any organization seeking to improve its understanding of DEI must approach this transformative journey with commitment, strategic planning, and a willingness to engage in continuous learning and adaptation for its staff and leadership.

As a Principal Innovation Consultant, a DEI Co-Chair, and an Organization Culture Leadership Architect, I have experienced excellent days when my team works hard to identify, understand, design, pilot, and implement solutions to what has been shared by staff members of organizations seeking improved work environments. I have also experienced days that feel deflating, painful, and unbearable due to organization inertia and the lack of adequate leadership support to help with the transformation organizations are seeking. I have conducted many DEI coaching and training sessions for practitioners who have stepped into these new roles and have been faced with similar roadblocks.

Many DEI practitioners step into these roles without sufficient budgets and supporting staff to help them carry out the vision, mission, and values of the organization that has hired them. These leaders quickly discover the expectation is for them to develop a Swiss Army knife mentality. They need to wear several hats and tackle many challenges that their stakeholders face on their own. When a culture architect starts feeling the insurmountable weight of the role they have to play with no sign of success, the idea of failure is crushing. In my coaching with them, they often say things like this:

- "I can't do this anymore; I fear the backlash in the media is creating a resistance to change at my organization."
- "This is my calling, but why am I losing my dedication and commitment?"
- "There are days I do not feel like going in to work or starting my own meetings, especially when nothing seems to be moving the needle of change."
- "Each time I share an idea or vision, my leadership team asks me for data or how I will quantify the results and the return on investment of my efforts."
- "I am experiencing diversity fatigue; my committee is overwhelmed, and I fear the media and atmosphere in the country are becoming desensitized to DEI efforts."

Hearing such quotes during coaching conversations often has me reflecting on what these accomplished leaders are facing and thinking that their inner saboteur's voice is telling them that they are a failure and an imposter who took an impossible task and had no chance of success. This natural feeling plagues many professionals who have been successful throughout their leadership careers because they often had different support structures. However, when assuming the DEI leadership role, they encounter new and foreign waters that require different leadership and negotiating skills that they need to unlock.

Recognizing the Signs

DEI practitioners need to recognize the signs of compassion fatigue early on to prevent its detrimental effects on their well-being and effectiveness. In leading organizational change, I have experienced emotional exhaustion from some of the staff's negative experiences, decreased empathy, irritability, cynicism, physical ailments, and a sense of helplessness or hopelessness when sharing the problems they face.

Over many projects, and in talking with colleagues trying to lead change in other organizations, I have identified several common factors that lead to compassion fatigue and burnout:

1. **Emotional Labor**
   DEI practitioners bear the emotional burden of individuals sharing experiences of discrimination, leading to emotional exhaustion and drain.
2. **Limited Resources**
   Insufficient resources such as time, budget, and personnel hinder practitioners from implementing meaningful change, contributing to stress and burnout.

3. **Resistance and Pushback**
   Overcoming resistance from individuals or groups who oppose DEI initiatives can lead to frustration and a sense of futility, exacerbating burnout.
4. **Role Strain**
   Balancing multiple roles as educators, advocates, and change agents while avoiding performative activism.
5. **Fear of Change**
   Resistance to DEI training often stems from a fear of change and discomfort with altering workplace dynamics or personal beliefs.
6. **Perceived Threat to Privilege**
   Discussions about privilege and power dynamics in DEI training can be perceived as a threat to personal advantages, leading to resistance.
7. **Misconceptions and Stereotypes**
   Preconceived notions that DEI training is unnecessary or biased, along with past negative experiences with such training, can fuel resistance.
8. **Feeling Personally Attacked**
   Confronting uncomfortable topics like bias or discrimination may make individuals feel personally attacked or misunderstood, leading to resistance.
9. **Inadequate Understanding of Relevance**
   Resistance may arise when individuals fail to see how DEI training directly impacts their work or daily

lives, highlighting the importance of demonstrating practical relevance.

10. **Fear of Making Mistakes**
    Fear of making mistakes or saying something offensive during DEI discussions can discourage engagement and hinder progress.

These are common and frustrating challenges, so if you are feeling any of these, you are not alone. In facing many of these myself, I have developed several practical strategies to build resilience and stay focused on my mission, vision, and values. The framework I've developed combines tools I've learned in professional coaching with experience from my international rugby career as a player, captain, and coach. Rugby is a complex sport that develops its athletes' mental and team collaboration capacity to overcome what is thrown at them during training, traveling to different countries, in learning the host's cultures, and during game situations.

Practical Strategies for Dealing with Compassion Fatigue

Developing sage powers based on the concepts of Positive Intelligence[1] can be transformational for DEI practitioners. These professionals often navigate complex and emotionally charged environments that can lead to high stress and burnout. The sage perspective, a core idea in Positive Intelligence, emphasizes activating a part of our brain that fosters more positive emotions and constructive interactions.

---
1   Chamine, Shirzad (2012). Positive Intelligence: Mental Fitness Program to Achieve Your True Potential. Perigee Trade. [positiveintelligence.com]

Here's how embracing sage powers can help DEI practitioners develop resilience and effectively combat burnout.

Understanding Sage Powers

As DEI practitioners in the U.S. face limited support, people need to develop their sage power. Sage powers involve accessing the deeper part of the brain that handles challenges with a positive mindset. The Positive Intelligence framework identifies five primary sage powers: empathy, exploration, innovation, navigation, and activation. Each of these powers can be harnessed to transform challenges into opportunities for growth and learning, which is crucial in the stressful field of DEI. As a professional coach, I help change leaders develop and tap into these powers in their own ways.

Empathy

Empathy, the ability to feel and understand others' emotions, is vital for DEI practitioners. This power helps in deeply understanding the experiences and feelings of individuals from diverse backgrounds. By developing empathy, DEI practitioners can create more inclusive and supportive environments. This emotional connection also helps mitigate the feelings of isolation that often accompany burnout, as practitioners feel a deeper connection to their work and its impact on real lives.

Exploration

Exploration involves an open-minded curiosity about possibilities without preconceived judgments. For DEI practitioners, this means being open to understanding diverse perspectives without bias. Exploration fosters a learning mindset, where challenges are seen as opportunities to learn rather than obstacles. This approach reduces stress and prevents burnout by focusing on growth and continuous improvement rather than dwelling on difficulties or perceived failures.

Innovation

Innovation in this context is about thoroughly understanding the problems, thinking outside the box, and finding creative solutions to problems. DEI work often requires innovative thinking to address systemic issues and implement effective change. By fostering innovation, DEI practitioners can find refreshing and fulfilling ways to achieve their goals, keeping their work dynamic and engaging, which is essential for avoiding burnout.

Navigation

Navigation involves choosing paths that work best for oneself and the organization. For DEI practitioners, this means identifying strategies that align well with personal values and organizational objectives. Effective navigation ensures that efforts are not only productive but also personally meaningful. This alignment reduces career friction and increases satisfaction, buffering against stress and burnout.

Activation

Activation focuses on taking decisive action and maintaining the motivation to follow through. For DEI practitioners, activation can mean implementing well-planned initiatives and seeing them through despite setbacks. This power is crucial for maintaining momentum and ensuring that DEI initiatives have a lasting impact, providing a sense of accomplishment and purpose that is vital for warding off burnout.

Combating Burnout with Sage Powers

Burnout among DEI practitioners can stem from constant exposure to resistance, slow progress, and the emotional labor of addressing ingrained prejudices and systemic issues. Leveraging sage powers enables practitioners to approach their roles with a mindset that seeks to understand, innovate, and find joy and satisfaction in complex work. This positive approach helps maintain high levels of engagement and commitment.

Furthermore, developing resilience through these sage powers involves shifting focus from what's going wrong to how challenges can be transformed into growth opportunities. Resilience is about bouncing back from setbacks with a stronger and more optimistic outlook. It's about seeing the value in every situation and learning from it, which is essential in the evolving field of DEI.

Rugby Leadership Framework

People can best develop their sage powers by studying their own personal life experience. I learned a tremendous amount during my years as an international rugby player, captain, and coach, that has helped me be a more resilient and effective change leader.

Rugby, often seen as a sport of physical toughness, is a game of mental resilience and strategic leadership. This high-intensity sport offers more than just athletic challenges; it provides profound life lessons, especially in resilience and leadership. As someone who has been on both sides of the game—as a player and a coach—I've witnessed firsthand how the principles honed on the rugby field are remarkably applicable to leadership in any field.

Rugby is more than just a game; it's a masterclass in teamwork and leadership. With its intense physical challenges and strategic depth, the essence of rugby mirrors the complexities of leading DEI initiatives in today's organizations. Both fields demand resilience, a deep commitment to team goals and tactics, and the ability to navigate through obstacles strategically. Here's how the sport of rugby can teach invaluable lessons in resilience for DEI leadership.

Resilience Through Continuous Play

In rugby, the play rarely stops; it continues through various challenges, be it weather, injuries, or setbacks. This relentless nature of the game teaches players to keep pushing forward, no matter the adversity. Similarly, in DEI or change leadership, the work is ongoing. Leaders face systemic barriers, resistance to change, and often slow progress.

Rugby instills the resilience needed to keep moving forward, emphasizing that setbacks are just part of the journey—not endpoints. It teaches DEI or change leaders the importance of perseverance and the strength of pushing forward even when the immediate results are not visible.

In the 80 minutes of a rugby game, teams must play two 40-minute halves, and at the end of the 80 minutes, the team that has accrued the most points wins the game. Our coaches had always instilled in the team the concept of continuous play, and during the 1997 Prescott Cup finals between St. Mary's Nairobi and Lenana High School, this was put to the test. The Prescott Cup is a prestigious rugby tournament in East Africa, specifically Kenya. It was named after A.A. Prescott, who was a headmaster at the Nairobi School (formerly known as Prince of Wales School) in the early 20th century. The tournament has a rich history and is one of the region's most significant schoolboy rugby competitions. The intensity mirrors the American Football High School Texas State Championship culture.

The Prescott Final is one that many young rugby players in East Africa and Kenya dream of, but only a few get to experience. The game started with me scoring the first try to take the lead 5-0 from one of the backline moves that had me the inside center, dummying Peter Ochola, the outside center, and Charles Cardovillis, the winger, freezing the defenders for a split second, which allowed me to display my speed to score a corner flag try. I missed the conversion from the right side of the field. An angle that was supposed to be easy for me due to the numerous repetition kicks I had been practicing for over three years. Missing points in a game full of slim margins often come back to haunt teams at the end of a game. Immediately after I missed the kick, I heard my captain, Mark Holi, bellow, "Tough luck, put it behind you."

Being analytical makes it challenging to brush things aside. From all the coaching I received, I knew these were the moments that define championships; I quickly registered that miss due to the fatigue from sprinting about 60 meters to score the try in the corner and then trying to compose myself for the kick at the mega Kenya Rugby Union field.

That was the only brilliant scoring opportunity we had in the first half. The team that was a well-oiled machine made some uncharacteristic mistakes that can be attributed to nerves of playing a championship game that saw a more disciplined Lenana punish our mistakes to tie the game 5-5, and then converted two penalties from a slip in concentration to take an 11-5 lead at the end of the half.

Teamwork and Diverse Strategies

At halftime, after a brief discussion of where we had challenges in our offense and what we could exploit from how our opponents played the first half, we made some changes to deal with the strong defense we faced. The team made room for the fastest winger, Gilbert Owour. Gilbert had beaten me in the 100-meter sprint at a track and field meet early in the week, and I finished second. Gilbert had not been featured much in our season campaign, and no team had filmed him. We knew we could utilize our hidden weapon, so we made the necessary adjustments to create space for our new winger.

Adapting to the Play

We needed to come out in the second half with an attacking mindset to win this game. The second half was tough; Lenana continued putting up a masterclass clinic on defending a team with a prolific offense with well-timed tackles throughout the second half. Only in the 77th minute of the game did we get our opportunity at the center of the field when I saw the Lenana winger had left a lot of space on his outside because he had no clue about the speed Gilbert possessed. I knew if we could hit Gilbert with a quick pass by missing both my centers, no one would catch him to the try line. The pass had to be perfect, and my centers needed to know I was skipping them and getting the ball to Gilbert. As I made the big pass, I shouted, "Miss two, miss two," and watched the spiral pass land in Gilbert's hands. The pass hit Gilbert in stride, and he beautifully stepped in and swerved out, forcing the defender to turn around and give chase.

The Saints fans and players who had just watched Gilbert be crowned the king of sprints early in the week got a chance to watch him again sprint, this time to score a critical try.

Learning from Each Play and Each Game

A rugby match is unpredictable, requiring players to adapt their strategies in real-time based on the opposing team's actions and the game's flow. This adaptability is crucial for changemakers in a continually evolving landscape.

As the Saints fans and my teammates celebrated joyfully, I didn't understand why Gilbert never scored closer to the posts to make the conversion kick manageable. Gilbert had his opponent well beaten and then scored the try at the worst section of the field, the corner flag where the Lenana fans were. This meant my kick preparation and concentration would be interrupted by yelling and heckling, a natural rugby ingredient that players responsible for kicking need to factor in at every game.

If I missed my first attempted kick, and that was absent of opponents' fan pressure, this kick had all the weight on it. As I jogged to pick up the ball to prepare for the kick, Captain Mark shouted, "We are down by one!" I looked at him and responded, "No, we are not!" That was me calming myself and beginning the process of calming my nerves down. If I missed that, the game would soon end, and we would lose by one point.

The Resilience to Push Boundaries

Rugby is about pushing physical and mental boundaries and challenging players to exceed their limits. DEI leaders (indeed, anyone trying to create change) must do the same—push the boundaries of traditional norms and policies to pave the way for more inclusive and equitable environments. Rugby teaches the courage to dig deep to find the strength to face challenges on and off the field. Changemakers must find and champion inspiration to challenge entrenched systems and advocate boldly for necessary changes.

In the three years of practicing my goal kicking, I played this moment in my head, and each time, I made this kick. I had even factored in the crowd distractions; however, I had yet to hear and experience the hostile rugby crowd of the opposition in person in a championship final. The kick was a meter from the touchline where the opposition fans stood. The noise and insults from the fans were relentless. The art of kicking in such an environment required me to forget my previous miss, ignore the noise from the opposition, factor the wind, and determine where to aim so the wind could put the ball where I wanted it to go.

Execution of the Plan

I took three deep breaths, and for the first time in my life, I managed to find my tunnel vision and ability to block out my internal saboteur and external noise. My mind calmed my nerves as it echoed softly, "You've got this, son, you've got this." That voice from my mind sounded like my father's calm, in-control baritone voice.

As I cautiously approached and struck the ball, the foot-to-ball connection was as smooth as poetry. I had experienced that kicking connection feeling for a long time, and I knew my kick was going in. I bent down to pick up the kicking tee I used to prop the ball off the ground and hand it to the Saints team bench. I looked at the faces of the noisy fans for a second, then glanced back at the ball still in flight, heading to its destination. The target was spectacular; the ball cleared the height of the crossbar with more than enough to spare, and it split the posts; the ball was in the dead center. The feeling of overcoming a challenge I experienced over 60 minutes ago and withstanding the pressure of the game and noise from the fans is one of my earliest lessons in finding ways to overcome obstacles you encounter. I have carried this with me through life, college, and career.

Nurturing Resilience

Both the rugged fields of rugby and the strategic realms of change culture leadership demand a unique blend of resilience, strategic foresight, and emotional intelligence. By drawing lessons from rugby's experiences and the nuanced approach of sage powers, DEI leaders can cultivate an environment ripe for transformation and enduring success.

Rugby teaches us the art of resilience and the importance of bouncing back stronger from every tackle and setback. It shows us that true strength lies not in never falling, but in rising every time we fall, ready to face the next challenge with greater wisdom and determination. This lesson is invaluable for DEI leaders who often navigate the complex dynamics of organizational cultures resistant to change. By embodying the resilience of a rugby player, DEI and change leaders can maintain their momentum and commitment, even when progress seems slow and fraught with challenges.

Moreover, rugby's emphasis on teamwork and diversity—where players with different abilities and roles synchronize to achieve a common goal—mirrors the essence of effective DEI and change initiatives. Just as a rugby team leverages the unique strengths of its players and the roles they play, organizations thrive when they embrace and utilize the diverse talents and perspectives of all employees. This inclusive approach not only enriches organizational culture but also drives innovation and performance, underscoring the practical benefits of a robust DEI strategy.

Developing sage powers enhances this journey by fostering a mindset equipped to handle the psychological and emotional demands of leading DEI efforts. The sage powers—empathy, exploration, innovation, navigation, and activation—equip leaders with the tools to transform challenges into opportunities for growth and learning. Empathy deepens our understanding and connection with others, fostering an inclusive culture that values each individual's contributions. Exploration encourages curiosity and openness, which are crucial for uncovering hidden biases and discovering transformative solutions. Innovation pushes the boundaries of what is possible, driving the systemic changes necessary for true equity. Navigation helps in making wise choices that align with both ethical standards and organizational goals, while activation propels these choices into action.

Lights on a City Wall

Laura Plato, MSc

Laura is CEO of The New Frequency, where she guides founders to the top 1% in the personal brand economy. She is a 2X professional certified life and well-being coach, a 5X CxO social impact technology executive, and a successful entrepreneur working at the intersection of social good and innovation. A nationally published author, speaker, and advisor, she has been featured on NBC, NPR, and CNN and in dozens of other media, including The New York Times, The Washington Post, and Good Housekeeping. She is a member of the Forbes Coaches Council. She served as Chair of the South Carolina Institutes of Innovation and Information Foundation, COO at SkysTheLimit.org, Chief Solutions Officer at VolunteerMatch.org, and COO at Causecast. She received her BA with Honors in English from Scripps College and holds an MSc in Criminal Justice Policy from The London School of Economics. She is a family caregiver.

Laura Plato, MSc

Nature's Nurture: Nature Connection in Caregiver Well-Being

The surgeon delivered the kind of mixed news I'd begun to grow used to receiving as the primary caregiver for my 79-year-old mother: today's exploratory procedure had gone pretty well, but the urgency was real. He was clearing his books to get her in for a complex intervention the following week that would be the actual test.

I thanked him, shook his hand, and watched him return to the OR. My blood was an odd cocktail of relief, anticipatory terror, and aching numbness. I felt hollowed out in the wake of waiting and worrying, and now this news (which was neither great nor terrible). I grabbed my things and bolted to the hospital's healing garden, subconsciously drawn to walk the labyrinth I knew lived there despite the freezing winter temperatures and the storm winds blowing in fresh snow. As I took my first steps, eyes on the pavers, I noticed the spindly, bare branches reaching toward me and the tufts of green herbs just peeking out despite the winter cold. I began to breathe again, and with each step, I could begin to believe it might be possible that my mom—that I—would be ok. Maybe not forever, but for right now. I was ok.

As caregivers, finding moments of tranquility and self-renewal can feel impossible—yet these moments are essential for avoiding compassion fatigue. In the labyrinth, observing the signs of resilience; on the walking trail, hearing the birdsong; in the garden, watching the bees dance; with the houseplants, tending to their needs and talking to them about the peace of growth and hope: these acts of being allied with nature bring a sense of profound peace and balance to my life as a caregiver, and I believe it is the essential element for all of us on this heart-centered journey.

The Caregiver's Burden

In the deeply personal realm of caregiving, an unspoken challenge often emerges: compassion fatigue.

Reflecting on my own experience while caring for my mother around the clock, I likened the emotional and physical exhaustion to an intense case of jet lag. It felt like I was divided into two selves: one acutely aware of my exhaustion, pleading for rest, and the other strangely detached, insisting on pushing forward to accomplish the tasks that stretched before me in an endless list. This fatigue was insidious, slowly enveloping me before I could even recognize it.

Balancing caregiving duties with my role as a Chief Operating Officer at an understaffed, growing nonprofit only compounded the difficulty. My mental state fluctuated wildly, from moments of hyper-lucidity to periods of lethargy where my thinking was cloudy and I struggled to remember even the simplest of facts. Ironically, as my mother battled aphasia, I found myself similarly at a loss for words, unable to articulate thoughts or solve problems that once came easily. My AirPods became my sanctuary, allowing me to focus on mundane tasks through ADHD focus music. Sleep eluded me. I cried at the drop of a hat. Anxiety was my constant companion. My husband wore a funny t-shirt that said, "Nobody cares – work harder." For better, for worse, it became my slogan.

I walked a tightrope, trying to remain composed with everyone around me—caregivers, my mother, my spouse, and doctors. One morning, my husband's simple, loving observation after an overnight vigil devastated me: "This can't continue. We have to find a better solution." Despite his unwavering support, I had never felt more alone or hopeless. I couldn't even find the words to respond. The guilt and anxiety—the sense I was failing everyone, everywhere, all the time—was suffocating.

This narrative is not unique to me. Many in the caregiving community face their own version of this dilemma. Compassion fatigue, with its complex blend of emotional and physical exhaustion, challenges us to find balance and seek healing, not just for those we care for but also for ourselves. Recognizing and naming this experience is the first step toward addressing it, opening a path to strategies and support that can alleviate the burden and restore our capacity for compassion and care.

The Healing Power of Nature: A Personal Reflection

For me, the answer arrived in getting back in touch with nature. Although I'm a confirmed couch potato who loves books and computers and hates the feeling of even a whisper of wind or a drop of rain on my face, nature now plays a profound and irreplaceable role in my life.

Engaging with the natural world—gardening, walking outdoors, and caring for plants and animals—has become my preferred antidote to the weariness and disconnection I experience as a caregiver. More than just a temporary respite, nature gives me the opportunity to reconnect with the Earth's energies, promoting a sense of connectedness and balance.

The practice of aligning with nature's subtle rhythms and patterns by fostering an intuitive interaction with the natural world is just that: a practice. There will be wind. There will be rain. But by gradually acclimating to this, I've learned that daily alignment brings a profound sense of peace and well-being. With its growth, decay, and rebirth cycles, my garden offers me a mirror to the cycles of caregiving and life itself, offering valuable lessons in resilience and renewal. Walking in nature, surrounded by simple sounds and movement, helps to quiet my mind and soothe my soul. For those times I'm simply unable to get outdoors, the act of caring for my houseplants or spending time with my pets rejuvenates and reignites the energy I have lost.

Aligning with the healing power of nature ultimately leads to greater fulfillment and satisfaction. The path to well-being and the mitigation of compassion fatigue lie in the soil, the sky, and the living things that surround and bind us.

The Healing Power of Nature: What the Research Tells Us

The notion that nature holds therapeutic benefits is far from new and certainly not my own discovery. Yet it is only in recent years that science has begun to unpack the mechanisms behind nature's healing powers. Research across disciplines consistently supports the idea that engagement with the natural world can contribute significantly to physical and emotional well-being. This body of evidence points to nature's role not just as a backdrop for leisure and recreation but as a vital component in the human capacity for healing and stress reduction.

Studies in environmental psychology have shown that spending time in nature or even viewing scenes of nature can reduce anger, fear, and stress while increasing pleasant feelings. Exposure to nature not only makes you feel better emotionally, but it also contributes to your physical well-being by reducing blood pressure, heart rate, muscle tension, and the production of stress hormones. According to scientists such as public health researchers Stamatakis and Mitchell, it may even reduce mortality.

One landmark study published in the *Journal of Environmental Psychology* found that individuals who simply walked in a natural setting reported lower levels of rumination—that pattern of negative, self-referential thought associated with a heightened risk of depression and anxiety—compared to those who walked in an

Nature-Centered Practices for Well-Being

The therapeutic benefits of nature can be harnessed through various practices that not only foster a deeper connection with the environment but also promote physical and emotional well-being. Gardening, walking meditation, and connecting in other simple, accessible ways such as tending to plants or caring for our pets, offer an effective means of combating compassion fatigue and enhancing life quality.

Gardening as a Practice for Wholeness and Health

Gardening offers incredible insights into cultivating a life worth living and fostering a deep sense of well-being. For me, it is more than a hobby or a means to beautify my surroundings. It's a form of meditation in motion, requiring focus, patience, and a gentle touch. Planting, weeding, and tending to my garden encourage mindfulness and presence, drawing my attention away from the incessant chatter in my mind and stress in my body and into a focused physical realm of soil, plants, and air. This shift in focus is inherently meditative and helps to promote a state of calm and centeredness.

From a physical standpoint, gardening promotes health through gentle exercise and exposure to fresh air and sunlight. So, if like me, you are not a massive fan of the treadmill or weightlifting at the gym, the physical effort involved in gardening activities such as digging, planting, and pruning can be a real gift—helping to improve cardiovascular health, flexibility, and strength while you're not even paying attention! It's a beautiful way to stay active while engaging in a nurturing and creative process.

I recommend beginning simply with a small project such as a container of flowers or a few potted herbs. Focus on the process rather than perfection. Celebrate your successes and learn from your failures. Gardening is, after all, a journey of growth, not just for the plants but for us as gardeners as well.

Walking Meditation: Steps Towards Inner Peace

Walking in nature combines the physical benefits of exercise with the mental and emotional benefits of meditation. Unlike traditional seated meditation, I've found that walking meditation allows me a greater freedom to make mistakes and recover. I don't put as much pressure on myself when I walk. Still, there is a deliberateness, a practice of being mindful and fully present while moving through the natural world, that I find unearths an essential and impeccable quality in my own thinking. This practice helps to quiet my mind, reduce stress, and foster a deep sense of connection with the world around me.

If you're new to walking meditation, my best advice is not to overthink it. Choose a natural setting for your walk, even somewhere familiar to you, if possible. Begin by standing still, taking a moment to notice your body and the sensations of standing on the earth. As you start to walk, focus on the experience of movement, paying attention to the feel of your feet touching the ground, the rhythm of your breath, and the sounds and sights around you. Allow thoughts to come and go without attachment, always bringing your focus back to the act of walking and your connection with nature. I suspect you'll notice your heartrate begin to decrease almost immediately.

My walks on my local trail, along the canyon, framed by ditch willows and set to the songs of wild birds, have been instrumental in my journey toward well-being. Often taken in silence, these walks allow me to step out of the cycle of worry and caregiving responsibilities, offering clarity and a renewed sense of purpose. The key is to be present, to stop once in a while and deepen your connection to your senses, to notice the life in and around you, and to let the natural world guide you back to your own inner peace.

Nature Connection: Beyond the Green Spaces

Connecting with nature can be challenging in urban environments. If you pause for a moment, you will notice nature is all around you, often in unexpected places, and finding ways to connect with it and realize its benefits can be much easier than you might think. I will admit I'm a bit over the top! I have assembled a collection of nearly 100 houseplants over the years. But what's amazing to me still is the intimate connection I feel to each and every one of these plants after living with them. I feel the energy of the new arrivals, and I know when the old guard is thirsty. It's a fascinating thing and a real reminder of how deeply intertwined we all are.

If you live or spend most of your time in urban settings, I urge you to take just a small break and allow yourself the freedom to

- Create a green space with houseplants, or a small stair or balcony garden in your home;
- Visit a local park or botanical garden regularly;

- Practice mindfulness or meditation outdoors, focusing on the natural elements around you, such as the sky, a tree, or a body of water; or
- Engage in citizen science projects such as bird watching or plant identification, to deepen to your connection to your local ecosystem.

Even in the heart of the city, these moments of connection offer a respite from the stresses of daily caregiving and provide a sense of belonging to the larger web of life. For me, tending to my collection of houseplants has been a way to bring nature indoors so that even in the dark cold of winter, my living space reflects the calm and resilience of the natural world. Each plant, with its unique needs and growth patterns, serves as a reminder of the diversity and complexity of life, offering me daily lessons in care, patience, and adaptability.

Incorporating nature-centered practices into our lives is not just a luxury but a necessity for our physical and emotional well-being. Gardening, walking meditation, and finding ways to connect with nature, even in urban environments, are accessible strategies that can help mitigate the effects of compassion fatigue and restore balance and peace to our lives.

Integrating Nature into Caregiving

Incorporating nature-centered practices in your daily caregiving routines can also enrich the lives of those you care for, offering sensory stimulation, a sense of connection, and opportunities for joy and engagement.

When you think about weaving nature into the fabric of caregiving, it's helpful to create routines and practices that are adaptable to various environments and schedules. Here are a few strategies I've used:

- **Create a Nature Routine**
  Dedicate a part of your day to engage privately with nature. This could be a five-minute morning walk, a 30-minute midday break in a nearby park, or a full evening tending to your pets, garden, or houseplants. The key is consistency and making this solo practice a non-negotiable part of your caregiving routine.
- **Bring Nature Indoors**
  For caregivers and care recipients who may have limited mobility or access to outdoor spaces, bringing elements of nature indoors can be incredibly beneficial. This can include setting up a window bird feeder to watch birds, tending to a collection of indoor plants, or even using natural materials for crafts and activities.
- **Use Technology to Connect with Nature**
  In situations where physical access to nature is challenging, technology can offer a bridge. Nature sounds and virtual tours of national parks or botanical gardens provide a powerful sensory connection to the natural world and can be wonderful ways to connect.

- **Adapt Activities to Abilities**
  Tailor nature-based activities to the physical and cognitive abilities of the care recipient. For example, someone with limited mobility might still enjoy sitting nearby, talking, and watching as you pot marigolds or arrange flowers, while individuals with more mobility can participate in short walks or light gardening tasks.
- **Incorporate Sensory Elements**
  Nature is rich in sensory experiences. I love to incorporate and encourage memory-making activities that engage the senses—from listening to bird songs to touching leaves or flower petals to smelling herbs or flowers and visually observing the diverse colors and movements of the natural world.

Sharing such activities with my mom brought unexpected moments of joy and connection. She had always loved gardening but had become increasingly disconnected from this passion due to her health challenges. When we shared peaceful moments together tending houseplants and a few pots of basil on the back step, she'd sit and advise me on the best way to plant up, water, trim, and even use our herbs to cook recipes she enjoys. This simple activity not only brightened her days but also provided us with a shared project that went beyond the usual care giver/care recipient dynamic, reinforcing our bond and offering us both a sense of healing and purpose.

I've heard similar stories from fellow caregivers. One friend shared how regular walks in a nearby park with her husband, who was dealing with dementia, seemed to awaken parts of him that had become less accessible. The sights and sounds of nature stimulate conversations, memories, and moments of clarity that are rare and precious.

To be clear, if you're feeling any resistance, integrating nature into your caregiving routine does not need to be about adding another task to your already busy schedule. It's about creating space for healing, connection, and joy amidst the challenges of caregiving. By adapting these practices to fit your individual needs and environments, you can find a powerful ally in nature, one that supports both your well-being and that of those you care for.

Practical Tips for Caregivers: Engaging with Nature

For caregivers looking to incorporate nature into their lives and the lives of those you care for, starting can sometimes feel daunting. However, engaging with nature doesn't have to involve grand gestures or significant changes to your daily routine. Here are some practical, accessible tips for integrating nature-centered practices into your caregiving journey, along with advice on overcoming common barriers.

Start Small

- **Indoor Plants**
  Begin with a low-maintenance houseplant or two. Plants like snake plants, pothos, and philodendrons are great starters. They require minimal care but can significantly

enhance the indoor environment, offering visual beauty and improved air quality.

- **Window Watching**
  Set up a comfortable space near a window where you and your care recipient can observe the outdoors. Watching birds, clouds, and leaves moving in the breeze or even the changing light can provide a sense of connection to the natural world.
- **Nature Sounds**
  Incorporate nature sounds into your daily routine. Many free apps and online platforms offer sounds like rain, forest, or ocean waves, which can be calming and restorative for both you and the person you're caring for.

Accessible Activities

- **Nature Walks**
  Short walks in safe, accessible areas can be incredibly beneficial. Even a stroll around the block or visiting a local park can offer fresh air and a change of scenery. If mobility is an issue, consider drives through scenic areas.
- **Gardening Together**
  Engage in simple gardening activities such as potting plants or creating a small herb garden on a windowsill. These activities offer sensory stimulation and the joy of nurturing life.

- **Nature Crafts**
  Collect natural materials like leaves, stones, or flowers for crafts. These can be as simple as arranging a small vase of flowers or creating a collage from fallen leaves.

Overcoming Common Barriers

- **Lack of Time**
  Incorporate nature into existing routines. For example, if you're sitting outside for a few minutes of fresh air, invite your care recipient to join you. Or listen to nature sounds while completing indoor tasks.
- **Urban Living**
  Seek out green spaces in your area such as community gardens, parks, or waterfronts. Many urban areas also have hidden gems like rooftop gardens, pocket parks, or greenways.
- **Physical Limitations**
  Adapt nature activities to be accessible. For example, bird watching can be done from a window, and many nature documentaries offer virtual experiences of the outdoors.
- **Mental Fatigue**
  Remember, the goal is to find rest and rejuvenation in nature, not to add another demanding task to your list. Choose activities that feel refreshing and manageable rather than overwhelming.

The key to successfully integrating nature into your caregiving routine is to view it as a companion on your journey—a source of comfort, strength, and renewal for you and the person you care for. Start with small steps, be open to exploring different activities, and adjust based on what feels most beneficial and enjoyable. Over time, you'll likely find that these moments of connection with nature become invaluable islands of peace in the busy caregiving sea, offering both you and your care recipient a richer, more balanced quality of life.

Why Invest the Time? The Broader Impact of Nature on Well-Being

The well-being of caregivers is a cornerstone upon which the health and happiness of those they care for rest. When caregivers harness nature's restorative power to enhance our well-being, the benefits extend far beyond our personal health, creating positive ripple effects throughout our immediate care environment and the broader community. The transformative potential of nature-centered practices on caregiving and personal health is real, and I want to take just a moment to zoom out and consider how these practices can help us all foster a more compassionate, resilient, and healthy society.

Enhancing Care Quality through Caregiver Well-Being

Caregivers who feel emotionally and physically replenished are more likely to provide high-quality, compassionate care. Nature's role in reducing stress and promoting mental clarity directly impacts caregivers' ability to remain present, patient, and attentive to the needs of those they support. This heightened level of care not only improves the quality of life for the care recipient but also strengthens the bond between caregiver and care recipient, fostering a more profound sense of trust and mutual respect.

Caregivers who engage in nature-centered practices often report a greater sense of fulfillment and purpose in our roles. This positive outlook can help to reduce feelings of burden and burnout, making the caregiving journey more sustainable and rewarding. As caregivers share our experiences and practices with colleagues, family members, and friends, we can inspire a wider adoption of nature-centered well-being strategies, promoting a healthier caregiving culture.

Ripple Effects on Care Recipients and Communities

The benefits of caregiver well-being extend to care recipients, who are likely to experience improved emotional and physical health outcomes as a result of receiving care from someone who is balanced, calm, and focused. This sense of enhanced care can lead to fewer health complications, a more positive outlook on life, and a stronger desire to engage in their own health and well-being practices.

The integration of nature-centered practices into caregiving can have significant implications for the broader community. Caregivers who find solace and rejuvenation in nature are more likely to advocate for green spaces, environmental conservation, and community wellness programs. This advocacy can lead to the development of more accessible natural areas, community gardens, and outdoor programs, benefiting the entire community by promoting a culture of health, sustainability, and interconnectedness.

Transforming Caregiving and Personal Health

The potential for nature-centered practices to transform caregiving and personal health is immense. By prioritizing our well-being through engagement with nature, caregivers can break the cycle of stress and burnout, leading to more compassionate, attentive, and effective care. This shift not only enhances the lives of caregivers and those we care for but also contributes to the creation of healthier, more resilient communities.

As society grapples with the challenges of an aging population and the increasing demands on caregivers, adopting nature-centered well-being practices offers a hopeful path forward. These practices provide a sustainable, accessible means of supporting caregiver health, improving care quality, and fostering a greater sense of community connection and well-being. In embracing the healing power of nature, caregivers can find the strength and balance needed to navigate our caregiving journeys with grace and resilience, setting a powerful example for all those touched by care.

While often challenging, the journey of caregiving holds the potential for profound growth and fulfillment. Nature, with its inherent capacity for healing and renewal, emerges as our vital ally in this journey, offering caregivers a source of strength, comfort, and rejuvenation. By turning to the natural world, caregivers can find respite from the demands of our roles, reconnect with our sense of self, and cultivate the resilience needed to continue providing compassionate care.

To all the caregivers embarking on this journey of integrating nature into your caregiving practice: please know that you are not alone. Being a caregiver is not always easy, but it is rich with opportunities for discovery, healing, and connection. Allow nature to be your guide and companion, offering its gifts freely and abundantly. Remember, in caring for yourself with the same compassion and dedication you give to others, you are not only enhancing your own well-being but also enriching the lives of those you care for and the broader community. May you find in nature a wellspring of resilience, peace, and joy to sustain you on your caregiving journey. And together, let us embrace the healing power of nature, forging a path toward a more balanced, connected, and compassionate world.

Way Out

Nayely Duran, ACC

Nayely is a dedicated consultant, trainer and executive leadership coach with over a decade of experience. Having worked with clients across various industries, Nayely brings a wealth of understanding and expertise to every engagement. Passionate about acquiring and sharing knowledge, Nayely takes pride in helping others strengthen their self-leadership, sharpen their skills, acquire tools for self-development, and embrace their inner power. Born in Mexico City and residing in San Francisco since 2009, Nayely combines a rich cultural heritage with a global perspective to deliver impactful and transformative coaching experiences. www.nayelyduran.com

Nayely Duran, ACC

Embracing Compassion Without Losing Yourself

During the pandemic, I found myself paying closer attention to the concept of compassion fatigue than ever before. Watching frontline workers on television tirelessly providing selfless and loving support to those in need was both inspiring and eye-opening. While doctors, nurses, and essential service providers were at the forefront of these efforts, it soon became apparent that the exhaustion, stress, and distress of exercising compassionate empathy could easily be extended to all of us. And, because compassion fatigue is certainly not a pleasant feeling, it's important to recognize that there is a way out, and there are strategies to build emotional strength to prevent it.

As human beings, we are wired to connect with others. Empathy is one of our instinctive ways of doing so—the ability to understand or feel what others feel. However, there's another layer to our empathetic selves: compassion. When we practice compassionate empathy, we not only seek to understand and feel as others do, but we also feel compelled to take action to help them through their difficulties.

While this is a healthy and humane reaction, we can become overwhelmed by the desire to understand, feel, and help others without setting boundaries. It's seen as a noble trait to care for others, but during the pandemic I began to question why it was causing so much hurt and distress.

In my process to find answers to those questions, I understood that it was imperative to review how my upbringings had shaped my mindset, paradigms, and values, and how these would play a role in compassion fatigue.

Fostering a Culture of Care by a Family-Oriented Society

"You should have kids. At least one. Otherwise, who is going to take care of you when you grow older?"

This refrain echoes through my memory, as I heard it often from women that shared my Latin-American culture. According to it, we are born into the responsibility of taking care of our parents. Growing up we learn soon enough that our ties with immediate and extended family are constructed by providing service to all of those who are sick, handicapped, or going through any rough situation.

Born and raised in the bustling metropolis of Mexico City, I was immersed in a society where familial bonds were revered. From the moment we enter this world, we are enveloped in the warmth of our extended family, each member playing a vital role in our upbringing. The concept of care extends far beyond the nuclear family, encompassing grandparents, aunts, uncles, cousins, and even neighbors. It is a collective responsibility—a shared burden and a shared joy—that supposedly binds us together in a tapestry of love and support.

Growing up, I vividly recall the rhythm of family life revolving around caring for our loved ones. Whenever one of my aunts or grandparents needed assistance, it sparked a mobilization within our family. I watched as relatives came together to ensure that each person received the care they needed. It wasn't uncommon to see my father spending nights in the hospital with a grandparent, only to have another relative take over in the morning, allowing him to rest. This cycle continued, illustrating the deep-rooted practice of caregiving within family-oriented cultures. From an early age, we are immersed in a culture that emphasizes the importance of caring for our family members, regardless of the closeness of our relationships or the distances between us. This ingrained sense of responsibility teaches us that looking after our family is not just a choice but a fundamental aspect of our identity.

Nurturing a Spirit of Service Through Religious Education

Growing up, my parents took us to church where they constantly held positions of leadership. Through their words and deeds, my parents did a great job teaching us at home about the true fulfillment that lies in the care for others.

In my family, faith was not just a set of beliefs; it was a way of life. We were taught to see God in the faces of our neighbors, to extend a hand of friendship to the stranger at our door.

I'll never forget one summer morning when I was only seven years old. I loved spending all my time with my father, and since I wasn't at school, I used to accompany him to work at least one day a week. But that morning, while we were driving to his work, he suddenly stopped the car. Without saying anything, he got out of the car. I followed him with my eyes and then saw him picking up a man who looked intoxicated, barely able to stand on his own. My dad carried this man back to our car. The sight of this man really troubled me. My dad seated him in the front seat and just told me, "We will need to make a stop before work."

I was afraid. I didn't know the man, didn't know if he was hurt or could hurt us. My father stopped at a small building that I now know was an AA group center, took the man inside, and after ten or fifteen minutes, he came back. I asked him, "Dad, who was that man? What happened to him?" My dad responded, "I don't know that man, but he needed our help." Then I asked, "Why do we have to help him?" My father replied, "Because we were in the right time and in the right place to do so."

My father didn't know that man, but he felt compelled to care for him. Without knowing it, he taught me that in life, we can blindly focus on our destination, or we can be aware of and attentive to those who are on the road with us.

The fusion of my parent's example with my cultural and religious teachings shaped my worldview, defining my role as a caretaker from an early age. It was a role I embraced wholeheartedly, for in caring for others, I found purpose, meaning, and a sense of belonging that transcended the boundaries of time and space.

Culture of Caring Across Miles

In 2009, I moved to San Francisco. Being an immigrant involves more than just physically leaving your homeland; it means enduring periods of mourning and grief that can last for years. The compassionate empathy instilled in you doesn't fade when you leave the place that nurtured you. Instead, the desire to stay informed about your loved ones' well-being and to care for those you miss intensifies, especially when you were raised with values centered on service, care, and love for others.

Grateful for the telephone, I never saw distance as an impediment to spending time with my parents and family. I used to talk to my parents daily, catching up on the day's events and enjoying a bit of *chisme*, our way of sharing family updates and stories. Occasionally, these conversations revealed difficult situations they or other family members were facing. Each time this happened, I felt a heaviness in my stomach and a strong urge to take action and help however I could.

This emotional response, I now understand, is known as vicarious trauma or secondary traumatic stress in the context of compassion fatigue. Even though I wasn't physically present, knowing that loved ones were going through tough times affected me deeply, making me anxious, sad, and tired.

The Other Side of Caregiving Philosophy

However, beneath the surface of this culture of care and the duty of religious belief lies a silent burden—an invisible weight that presses down on our shoulders, unnoticed yet ever-present. It is the expectation, subtly ingrained in us from birth, to prioritize the needs of others above our own. From the subtle nudges of societal norms to the weighty expectations of family traditions, we are conditioned to believe that selflessness is the pinnacle of virtue, the ultimate expression of goodness and worthiness.

This unspoken mandate permeates every aspect of our lives, weaving itself into the very fabric of our existence. It dictates the choices we make, the sacrifices we endure, and the boundaries we set—or rather, the boundaries we fail to set. For in a culture that venerates selflessness above all else, the act of prioritizing our own needs can feel like an act of betrayal, a betrayal not only of those who depend on us but of the values and beliefs that define us.

Providing tireless service and care to others can be accompanied by the pressure to conform to the rules, fear of judgment and disapproval from society, fear of disappointment and rejection from our loved ones, and perhaps most insidiously, fear of the guilt and shame inflicted by our own religious beliefs. It is this fear that may be driving some of us to the brink, to exhaust ourselves in the relentless pursuit of perfection, sacrificing our own well-being on the altar of duty and obligation. And yet, in our zeal to serve others, we risk losing sight of our own humanity—of the fragile, fallible beings that we are.

A Breakthrough

One of the lessons I learned from 2020 was the awareness it brought me regarding my self-care practices. Although I thought I was taking good care of myself, I realized that I was actually putting myself in second place. Throughout that year, my focus on caring and worrying about the well-being of others left me feeling broken.

The year 2020 will always be remembered for the events surrounding COVID-19. We heard the authorities declare a pandemic, saw the increasing number of deaths, and feared for the safety of our loved ones. From the onset of the pandemic, I found myself buying supplies for my parents, ordering oximeters from Amazon for family and friends, and constantly checking in on their physical and emotional well-being. I was determined to support everyone in any way I could. I participated in prayer circles, joined Zoom meetings to help combat loneliness, and volunteered to assist vulnerable groups such as the elderly and immigrants. I repeatedly assured others that I was there for them, ready to support and help in any way possible.

Later that year, however, I experienced my first panic attack. It caught me completely off guard. Just days before, I had expressed my feelings of exhaustion, stress, and worry to a friend, stating that I didn't want to feel that way anymore. When she asked how I would wish to feel, my immediate response was, "I want to feel rested, as if someone has my back, and I want to find peace in my heart."

Sometimes I wonder if that conversation was a message I inadvertently sent to the universe, and the panic attack was its response urging me to stop. A panic attack feels like losing control over everything, as if something is looming and you're powerless to stop it. You sense your power and control slipping away, leaving you vulnerable as your emotions and thoughts are sucked into a void. It was in that moment that I realized I had been neglecting myself for far too long, failing to care for myself in the way I needed. I had been ignoring my own need for rest and attention, prioritizing others over myself.

While those I helped throughout my life never asked for my assistance, the act of serving and empathizing had become so deeply ingrained in me that it became my identity. I felt it was the only way I knew how to operate, especially in such challenging times.

Then, I realized that I had rarely asked for help myself. While I had always sought the guidance of therapists and mentors, I never truly relied on my close support network. This realization made me aware of how much I had neglected my own well-being while caring for others. I now appreciate this awareness, as it has allowed me to live my authentic self without causing harm to myself.

As a professional coach, I've encountered compassion fatigue across various walks of life—among parents, sons and daughters, managers, executives, and entrepreneurs. The first step in addressing this is to recognize that the feelings arising from compassion fatigue are valid.

You might have wondered, "How can I continue caring for those I love without harming my mental and emotional health? Is that even possible?" While caring for others, it's crucial to avoid reaching the breaking point by making changes to protect your well-being. It's essential to untangle the beliefs and misconceptions we may have about empathy, compassion, and caring for others.

Five Strategies to Navigate Compassion Fatigue

One of the most deceptive aspects of compassion fatigue is its ability to blur the boundaries between selflessness and self-neglect. When we have convinced ourselves that our worth is measured by our capacity to give, we can't see the warning signs of burnout until it's too late.

Here are five important strategies I use to heal from compassion fatigue while living a life with authentic love, care, and kindness:

Unwind Your Narrative

After my panic episode, the first thing I committed to doing was understanding what led me to it. How was it possible that wanting the best for others and helping them could harm me in this way? With the help of my therapist, I was able to find the answer to that question. It's key not only to resolving compassion fatigue but also to handling any other emotions or situations life may throw at you.

The issue behind my compassion fatigue was the narrative I held about love, care, and service. There's an innate kindness within me, but I had learned early on to interpret service and the idea of "loving your neighbor" as a means to earn my place in the world, to belong, to find my worth, and to be loved. Initially, acknowledging this brought a sense of shame and self-judgment because I felt I should have found self-worth internally. However, upon further reflection, I realized that this way of living was not intentional but reactive to what I was taught over the years. And that fact didn't negate my genuine love for service and caring for others. I just needed to recognize my own reality and rewrite my narrative around it. In doing so, I was able to reclaim my history and empower myself to move forward with autonomy and on the path of my own agency.

Ask yourself this question: What in your life is shaping the way you care for others and the ways you are caring for yourself (or not)? Engage in this honest exercise with yourself. If you don't currently have professional help like a therapist or a counselor, you can also journal about it. What matters here is your self-awareness and providing an objective space to observe your narrative. Only from there you will be able to change it.

Build Safety Guardrails

Create an inventory of the things you've stopped doing for yourself in favor of others' well-being. This is important because as caregivers, we rarely pause to ask ourselves what *we* need. For example, I used to use almost all of my own vacation time to care for others rather than myself, and I often interrupted my happy state of mind by worrying about people or situations that weren't even within my reach to help. Making this list of even tiny things I was denying myself gave me a clearer picture of the areas I was neglecting.

Then, I made a conscious decision to list my non-negotiables when it came to serving others. These are the things we value so much that from now on, we're willing to protect them no matter what. For me, those were my inner peace, my self-respect, and the power to choose intentionally what I want to do. Your non-negotiables will become the guardrails that protect your authentic self, your well-being, and your integrity. When I feel the urge to help or worry about something or someone, or when I'm caring for someone who's ill or in a difficult situation, I now do it better, not only because I know how to not compromise on my three non-negotiables, but I am fully present when I help, and I can give others a better version of myself.

Practice Self-Compassion

Show up for yourself with compassion. While the word "compassion" implies empathy, it goes beyond just understanding or sympathizing with others; it's the stage where we feel compelled to mobilize that sentiment and act. Self-compassion is taking action to care for yourself. If you're feeling exhausted, tired, grumpy, or misunderstood, or if you're going through a tough situation like illness, a temporary or permanent disability, or just a rough patch that's hard to navigate, it's crucial to allow yourself the space to acknowledge what you're going through and then take action to care for yourself.

One of the things I did in my own recovery and for a better understanding of caregiving was to give myself what I thought I needed. This included many things, from therapy, physical exercise, and a general health checkup to taking more sunbaths, drinking my favorite tea, bringing back simple activities that I knew would spark my joy. I also had more conversations with trusted family members and friends where I could talk about myself. Yes, for those that are givers, we are also listeners, and it may be hard to talk about ourselves. But that will help us heal faster.

It takes a conscious change in mindset, but believe me, once you start feeling better, you'll be in a much-improved position to support others from a healthier standpoint. Remember, taking care of yourself isn't selfish; it's essential for your well-being and your ability to care for others effectively.

Build Your Trust

The fourth strategy is so helpful that it works even if you would skip the first three. It's about finding, exercising, and strengthening your trust. Beyond trusting yourself, seek to trust those around you and trust in something higher than yourself. When I talk about trusting those around you, I mean this: recognize that every person has the strength, the resources, the abilities, the gifts, and the resourcefulness to solve, heal, navigate, understand, embrace, accept, and deal with whatever situation they are going through. I'm not suggesting abandoning people to their luck during tough times, but rather acknowledging that they are capable of being the agents of their own lives.

With compassion fatigue comes the concept of "vicarious feeling," meaning you can experience sadness, anguish, fear, worries, or other emotions just by watching or hearing someone else's situation. Your body doesn't differentiate; it feels the emotion regardless, and this can significantly affect your well-being. However, trusting that those you feel you need to care for are also powerful beings can help alleviate that burden. They can manage. They can be as resourceful and resilient as you have been in your own life. Moreover, trust that there are others who want to help but may not have acted because you seemed to have everything "under control."

When I had that panic attack, I was visiting all my family in Mexico City. It happened the night before I was flying back to California. We had gathered to celebrate being together, laughing, playing games, and singing karaoke all day, so my episode came as a huge surprise to all of us. After I managed to calm down a bit, my family had some questions for me that I managed to answer.

They wanted to know what was happening to me, what triggered my situation. I mentioned many things that were constantly worrying me: their overall well-being due to the pandemic, my father's delicate health at the time, and other issues that were a huge concern for my mother, which started affecting her health.

After hearing this, each person in my family shared their support, not only with kind words for me but also with specific ways they would help in the situation. Some even mentioned that they had never considered themselves able to help, but they wanted me to know they could and were asking me to allow them to help. Letting them help me made them feel trusted and valuable as well.

Along the same lines of trust, it can be important to find spiritual support. Regardless of your beliefs, whether you are religious or believe in something else, it always helps to know that there is something else out there, something more perfect, wise, and skillful than you, especially something that knows and sees beyond what you can see. This higher power can take the wheel when you are tired, not only because you are loved but because everyone is worthy of that love.

Let Go of Control

Take time to review what role "control" is playing in your fatigue. In my case, I questioned the origins of my relentless need to protect everyone around me. Who told me it was my responsibility to shield them from harm? In this moment of self-reflection, I uncovered a profound realization—the people I cared for were resilient and capable of navigating challenges on their own. The burden of constant vigilance and control was not only unnecessary but detrimental to my own well-being.

In letting go of this illusion of control, I found liberation in trust and faith. Trusting in the inherent strength and resourcefulness of those I loved, and having faith that they would rise to meet any challenges that came their way. It was a profound shift that allowed me to reclaim my own sense of peace and vitality, and to cultivate a healthier, more balanced approach to caring for myself and others.

There comes a point where caring for others can morph into a toxic burden, a weight that drags us down. True love for others is not about controlling their every move; it's about believing in their capability, their intelligence, and their independence. It's about recognizing that everyone deserves the autonomy to live their own life, even if it means making mistakes along the way. Their life belongs to them, not to us.

Embracing this truth requires letting go of the illusion of control—a daunting task that may feel foreign and uncomfortable at first. Yet, once we release our grip, we're left wondering why we clung to control in the first place.

There is a video that circulated in social media few years ago. It was distressing imagery of a child desperately clutching a rope in a river, convinced that letting go would signify a disgrace for him. As the fear consumes him, it drains his energy and clouds his judgment. It's a vivid metaphor for how we can become consumed by a singular need to control things.

But then, as the camera pans down, we see the water barely reaching the child's waist, revealing the truth: his fears were unfounded. Similarly, when we relinquish control, we often discover that our efforts were misguided and unnecessary… but exhausting, nonetheless.

For me, letting go of control was a revelation—a shift from a hurtful form of caretaking to a more enlightened path. It's about planting your feet firmly on the ground, trusting in the resilience of others, and nurturing your own spirituality along the way.

Transformation

In reflecting on my journey through the pandemic, I've come to understand the profound impact of compassion fatigue on my life and well-being. The relentless urge to care for others, deeply ingrained through cultural, familial, and religious teachings, brought me to a breaking point. It was only through a personal crisis that I realized the importance of setting boundaries, practicing self-compassion, and trusting in the resilience of others.

The lessons learned from this experience have been transformative. Recognizing the validity of my feelings, untangling deep-rooted beliefs about empathy and care, and prioritizing my own needs have allowed me to find a healthier balance. As a professional coach, I've seen similar patterns in others and understand that we must change our narrative around care and compassion.

By unwinding our internal stories, building safety guardrails, practicing self-compassion, trusting in the strength of others, and letting go of control, we can navigate the complexities of compassion fatigue. These strategies not only prevent burnout but also enhance our ability to care for others from a place of genuine well-being.

Ultimately, embracing self-care is not an act of selfishness; it is a vital practice that enables us to support others effectively and sustainably. As we move forward, let us honor our own needs and recognize that true compassion begins with ourselves.

A Crutch on the Sidewalk

Dennis Brozzo, PMP

Dennis Brozzo is an executive leadership and life coach who spent 25+ years in Big Tech. Starting as a mailroom clerk, he rose through the ranks to positions of global leadership. After becoming a widower at age 47, he embarked on the second chapter of his life. Through his journey of grief and recovery, Dennis discovered his life's calling: to help others successfully navigate their own life-changing events. As a coach, he works with individuals who desire transformative growth in both career and personal spaces, supporting them in building fulfilling lives for themselves. When he is not coaching, Dennis can be found enjoying many outdoor activities, as well as playing the saxophone, writing, volunteering for causes near to his heart, and building his own fulfilling life with his new wife. Look for Dennis at vertoC2LLC.com.

Dennis Brozzo, PMP

On Love, Loss, and Recovery from Devastation

In February of 2019, I began to witness my wife, Michelle, experience strange abdominal pain. At first, we assumed it was a passing case of indigestion, or maybe an ulcer triggered by the stress of being an entrepreneur. As each day passed, though, her pain grew more intense. Michelle wasn't fond of modern medicine or going to the hospital, so we spent several weeks researching every homeopathic remedy we could find for gastric ailments. No matter what we tried, the symptoms just got worse. Finally, after an incident of violent vomiting and fainting, I rushed her to the emergency room. The ER doctors suspected an ulcer and sent Michelle home with a prescription for an acid reducer and an appointment to see her regular doctor the next week. We spent the weekend at home as I tried to reduce her discomfort the best I could. On Monday morning, as Michelle was getting ready for her appointment, she collapsed in the bathroom and was once again rushed to the ER.

We spent that day in the ER, surrounded by doctors and nurses, with no answers. My wife had IVs in each arm, received cocktails of drugs, endured two blood transfusions, and made multiple trips to every imaging department in the hospital. The doctors suspected the worst-case scenario but did not tip their hand until more tests were performed and Michelle was fully checked into the hospital. Because Michelle was an intensely private person, I knew that she did not want me to inform any family or friends at this point. This meant that I was running in and out of the hospital to work remotely from the car and running home every four hours to take care of our pets. Once Michelle was finally checked in to the hospital that evening, I had my first opportunity to slow down, and I slept on the floor next to her bed. In retrospect this was the first sign that I would need an entire team to support my wife on this journey. Try to pay attention to the early signs in your own situation. Instead of trying to be an army of one, be one of an army that can help with all the various aspects of the crisis.

The following day, Michelle continued to be poked and prodded and given a plethora of tests. I said to myself, "I have no idea how to handle this! What's going on? What is my place here? What's the right thing to say in the hard conversations?" To answer these questions, I kept giving myself the pep talk of all pep talks: "Your life has been built on finding the strength to overcome adversities. You're a gladiator! You've got this! You would even be able to handle it if your hair were on fire!" As clueless as I was at this point, I believed I would need to be the perfect foundation of support for everyone, everywhere, all the time. I was wrong, but it took me a long time to realize that. Your physical, mental, and emotional health is just as important as that of the person you're caring for. Seek support for yourself so you can be strong for your loved one when you need to be.

At the end of Michelle's first day in the hospital, we received the diagnosis: Cancer. We wanted to get started on treatment right away, but the tumor was blocking Michelle's intestinal tract and effectively starving her to death. She needed to be nourished right away, and the doctors recommended inserting an intravenous catheter, or PICC line, in Michelle's arm to administer nutrition. However, they said this was a high-risk option that might result in bleeding, nerve injury, irregular heartbeat, damage to veins in the arm, blood clots, or infection.

This absolutely freaked us out, and she was against it. The side effects could destroy her ability to be a jewelry designer and metalsmith—her passion in life. The doctors, with the best of intentions, tried to tell, almost command, Michelle to accept the PICC line, but being strong-willed, she dug in her heels. As one doctor after another tried to convince her, we were at an impasse, and I felt like crawling up the walls in frustration. I was overwhelmed and not thinking clearly, until I remembered that one of the best defenses against uncertainty was curiosity. Confronting the doctors, I asked what the alternatives were, percentages of risk, and what the likely outcomes would be. One doctor eventually laid it out clearly enough: While the side effects were significant, the probability of those side effects was low. Not having the PICC line, however, would mean a 100% risk of dying. With that understanding,

Michelle finally allowed the PICC line, which got her healthy enough for surgery.

I've always been the person who gets things done and avoids confrontation by being the mediator or negotiator. In that first week of information overload and disagreement, I was tested like never before and almost lost my grace. At the same time, I was still trying to get my day job done and take care of the household. I was at my wits' end. I was physically and emotionally exhausted, getting only a couple of hours of sleep each night. Being driven by my love for Michelle, I would have cracked skulls to do whatever was best for her, but I had to keep my cool so that I could fulfill my role as a caregiver and advocate. When you're looking death in the face, repeating the mantra "Keep calm and carry on" only goes so far. I was learning a new lesson in life: to take on any uncertainty, one needs to remember to be cool-headed and curious. Finding ways to give yourself space to get to that calm, cool, curious place isn't easy, but it helps both you and your loved one make your way successfully through the crises that arise. I also had to dig deep for the emotional and spiritual strength to care for Michelle, and still find ways to care for myself. I did some things right, and I did some things very, very wrong.

Making it through the first month, we finally got to the day of Michelle's surgery and the arrival of her parents. With more players in the mix, things got a lot more complicated; I had to juggle being Michelle's care advocate with being a mediator between her parents and the medical staff. At every bedside visit, her parents would pepper the doctors with questions, looking for answers about treatment and prognosis. Doctors can be evasive when answering questions, not wanting to be held to absolutes. Not getting straight answers drove all of us bonkers, especially Michelle's parents. The only way I could defuse the confrontations was to escort one or the other of her parents outside for "a breath of fresh air," our code for having a cigarette. In hindsight, this would have been a great opportunity to make Michelle's parents part of *my* care team, my "army," instead of trying to manage everything myself. Not being perfect is perfectly acceptable, especially in times of crisis. Unfortunately, I still had to learn that we all need help: Just prior to Michelle getting sick, I had successfully quit a twenty-year nicotine addiction and remained smoke-free through that first month of mayhem. I succumbed to the stress by indulging in the joy of smoking, which eventually led me to another five years of nicotine addiction. Turning to toxic crutches may seem like what you need in the moment, but in the long run it will cost you more than you realize.

After a week in the hospital, Michelle came home to start long-term recovery. The first big surprise was that my mother-in-law made a unilateral decision to move in with us. In addition, after a month of bed rest, Michelle was healthy enough to start chemo… but it came with a second, more gut-wrenching surprise: Even though the surgery had completely removed the primary tumor, a whole new cluster of cancers had developed. Now, instead of having the one tumor removed followed by a couple of months of chemo, Michelle was faced with six new tumors embedded in her liver. A second surgery was not viable, so the next course was heavy-duty chemo with the hope it would eradicate the tumors. I was shocked and worn out, but it was time to muster emotional strength and energy for another round of supporting my wife.

As we discussed the treatments, she almost refused chemo because of the possible side effect of peripheral neuropathy. Losing any functionality in her hands absolutely terrified Michelle. Her hands were her single-most important tool in being an artist, and without that she would rather not live at all. This also terrified me. On one hand, I too did not want my wife to live an unfulfilling life, but at the same time I still wanted her to live, artistic expression be damned. I was now faced with trying to convince Michelle to take the path of life over the loss of it. My approach was to empower her own agency. I made the argument that she could choose to go forward with the chemo, but at any time, if the neuropathy began to appear and she was unhappy with it, she could choose to stop that specific treatment and demand a switch to another drug or chemo cocktail. Because of that, Michelle chose to start chemo with the confidence that if the result did not satisfy her, she had the power to choose another path.

This was also an important lesson. As much as I wanted to run the show and make all the decisions, I had to learn to accept that some decisions were not mine to make. It was a tough truth to swallow, but one that was for the best. When the decisions become more difficult, and there is nothing you can do to change the circumstances, it's important to try to be at peace with the wishes of your loved one and even, when it's needed, to accept their fate as it is.

With chemo underway and my mother-in-law settled in, you would think things would be going better. Her presence in our home, however, doubled my caregiving burden. Michelle's mom's energy would often overwhelm me many days, and my wife's steadfastness would drive her mom crazy. Also, Michelle was still very lethargic as her pain killers and drugs to control the chemo's side effects caused her to sleep many hours of most days, and I was back to working full-time.

Her mom, on the other hand, was whipping up a handful of projects. As a person who was always in motion, she would look for things to do around the house to keep herself busy. For the next several months, she engaged in an array of DIY projects. Striving to be the perfect son-in-law, I acquiesced and fulfilled her every request. Michelle had a vision for how she wanted things to turn out, but her mother had her own opinions and vision. As the projects progressed, I had to ensure that they were done to Michelle's satisfaction. To avoid arguments and relieve Michelle's aggravation and tension, I jumped into the middle of every project, acting as a buffer between Michelle and her mom. It stressed *me* out, both having to take care of a whole new workload and having to stay calm in the midst of household tension. Adding a layer to the social and emotional fatigue, I was so busy managing everything during the day that I started working nights—I was getting what medical science would consider an abysmal amount of sleep to even function. As the months went on, her mom was creating a chasm between me and Michelle, taking me away from what I considered to be the most important task of a caregiver: being at my loved one's side.

In the process of caring for my wife, I took on and absorbed all her stress, anxiety, frustration, and terror all the while having no release for what I was going through. About six months after Michelle's diagnosis, I began to experience excruciating chest pains and shortness of breath. This initially happened every few days but escalated to multiple times a day. Exactly what the chest pains were, I will never know, because—foolishly—I kept them secret. I knew something was gravely wrong and that things had to change if I wanted to have a hope of being there for Michelle at the end. This is when I stepped back and looked at the situation. What could I do? No more household projects, no more sleep deprivation, no more managing household tension: it was time to ask Michelle's mom to go home. Her mom's help was needed at critical times, but the continued stay was having a longer-term detrimental effect. Anticipating a difficult conversation, Michelle and I framed it positively rather than negatively, in the context of Michelle's most important needs: peace, solace, and a slower pace. The best "help" her mom could provide was *not* to "help," and allow us to get back to a slower, more peaceful life. Using that framing, the conversation went well, and Michelle's mom went back to her own life. By now, all I wanted to do was collapse with exhaustion, but I didn't have that luxury. Instead, I slowed down to Michelle's pace. I continued to work, but I stopped trying to be an overachiever and did the bare minimum at my job. Although the first six months of chemo showed signs of success, we entered the next phase of the journey.

Over the next six months, chemo fatigue began to set in. I saw Michelle getting tired and frustrated with the physical toll it took on her mind and body, and watched her energy diminishing to the point where she was not able to do any of the normal things she enjoyed most. In addition, I could tell she began to dread going to chemo and continuing to endure the treatments. As the months went on, she began to realize, deep down, that the cancer was going to win. I later learned that she kept going through chemo so we could have as many months together as possible, no matter how it played out. In those months, she saw the toll caregiving was having on me, and she cleverly gave me an "order" that made her happy, and which provided me with an opportunity for self-care. Prior to Michelle's cancer diagnosis, we would take our dog, Winston, for a group dog walk on the beach. Seeing Winston filled with playfulness and energy was a weekly highlight for us. My wife knew that by taking Winston to the beach, it would give me a break from caregiving, allow me to experience a couple hours of joy, and not feel guilty about Michelle remaining home. It helped me recharge my batteries so I could keep going.

On a day-to-day basis during Michelle's waking hours, I was at her side with little else taking priority. We binge-watched her favorite TV shows, did jigsaw puzzles, cuddled with our dog and cats, talked about life in the present, and reminisced about our happiest moments together. At the rare times when she was strong enough to leave the house, we would plan an occasional date night, go for drives down the Pacific coast, or go to the local park and admire the ducks swimming around the pond, all the while exchanging abundant *I love you*'s. Making the decision to slow down was the best thing I did. Taking the time to focus on Michelle's peace and solace was the most important thing for me. When she had that, it gave me the fuel to re-focus my energy and keep going, even though I didn't have outside support.

On the one-year anniversary of Michelle's diagnosis, the world changed forever with the outbreak of COVID-19. Completely isolated from the world, I was running on fumes with no reprieve. Worse, I was no longer allowed to sit beside my wife during chemo infusions. For her last six chemo infusions, which took place in the early months of the pandemic, Michelle's dread was so deep that I had to carry her in my arms out to the car. Seeing her tears crushed me. I had bottled it all up, believing that if I started to break down, Michelle would worry about me, which would add to her hardship. Resolving to not let that happen, I made it a point to absorb any pain or suffering she expressed. Although no one was there to relieve me, I took the time during her infusions to drive across town to my favorite fly-fishing shop and dream about stress-free times. On my way back, I'd buy flowers and chocolates at the grocery store, which always put a huge smile on my wife's face. Taking an occasional sliver of time for myself, and creating small moments of kindness, helped me to power on.

As the last round of chemo ended, the most devastating of all appointments had finally arrived. The oncologists diagnosed Michelle's cancer as terminal. This meant the possibility of checking into a hospice facility or the hospital for end-of-life care. At the height of COVID-19 checking into a hospital for end-of-life care really meant dying without loved ones at your side. Michelle refused to enter any facilities and resolved to live the rest of her life at home. There was no way she was going to take her last breath without me at her side, and I did not care what I had to do to fulfill that wish, even it meant my own demise. With the guidance of the hospice care doctors and nurses, I did everything at home, in isolation. I was on the phone at least once week talking to doctors about pain management and making what felt like a never-ending rush to the pharmacy for the next most powerful pain medications.

In her last three months, Michelle slept almost 18 hours a day. There was very little for me to do except sit at her bedside, providing whatever she needed. When she was asleep, I would lay my hand on her side and meander through the labyrinth of my mind, recalling all that had happened and pondering what was to come. Every day was filled with moments of joy in remembering amazing experiences from the past, and hours of tears knowing that I would never experience that kind and love and happiness with her in the future. Thinking about a future without her was devastating and left me with a lack of desire to live on.

On one of those quiet days, we had a conversation that would change my life forever. Calling me into the bedroom, Michelle shared one of several dying wishes. It was important to her that I not spend the rest of my life alone and in grief. She stated in no uncertain terms that she wanted me to go out in the world and find love again. Not expecting this dying wish, I replied that I had absolutely no desire to love anyone else except her for the rest of my life, but I promised her that I would dedicate the rest of my life to doing something that would honor her memory and the legacy of love she gave to me and the world around us. At the time, I had no idea what that "thing" would ultimately be, but making that promise gave me an infusion of strength to endure the remainder of Michelle's life as well as the fortitude to persevere as a widower after she was gone. This one conversation was so meaningful to me that it led to me completely rethinking my future, crafting my life into one of helping others through their own journeys, including addressing compassion fatigue and grief.

Near the end, my wife wanted her dearest friends to visit from out of town. I was also working longer hours on my job to meet my deliverables ahead of schedule so that I could take time off at a moment's notice without having to worry about work when I was gone. It was clear that the visits from friends were a roller coaster of emotions for everyone. Each person had private moments with Michelle at the end of their visit to say their final goodbyes. After the last of those visits, I saw that Michelle's body began to shut down, and in the final seven days, her ability to interact with the world began to diminish. Soon, when she was awake, we could not exchange words; we would connect by looking deeply into each other's eyes, talking to each other only through the magic of the love we had for each other. On that final night, as I held Michelle in my arms, at the moment of her dying breath, I felt a sense of my own death. Half of my heart, my soul, and the center of my universe was gone. It felt like I had nothing left to live for and no reason to live. In that moment, I felt fully the devastation that the past 20 months of my life had wrought on me, and the intense compassion fatigue that had set in over that period.

Moreover, I was unprepared for "widow grief." In the widow community we say that the loss of a spouse is the hardest kind of grief. The reason is that the person from whom you need the most help in the grieving process is the person for whom you are grieving to begin with, and there is no replacement for the person you have lost. I can state with certainty that there is nothing that can prepare a person for that kind of loss.

Michelle's death was the trigger, releasing everything I had been suppressing all that time. Mind you, I had not bottled *everything* up; realistically that is just not possible. I had, however, suppressed far more than I realized. After her loss, I learned new things that I wish I had previously known. Clinically speaking, a person who is suffering from compassion fatigue can sometimes experience a phenomenon known as "psychic numbing." This is the act of dialing down one's empathetic instincts while caregiving, freeing up cognitive resources to find solutions to the immediate problems.[1] Throughout the journey I was so busy solving one problem after another that any compassion I could muster was given entirely to Michelle, and I failed to have any compassion for myself. Ironically, that reduced the amount of compassion fuel I had available in my tank to give back to my wife. Everyone around me said, "Dennis, you need to take care of your mental health," but my standard reply was "Sorry, no time. I'll take care of it after Michelle is gone." I was unknowingly developing a layer of psychic numbing that would make it harder for me to find my way forward. During this journey I had contained my emotions to a very narrow spectrum that were only relevant to my job as a caregiver. For a vast majority of the time, I completely buried my emotions as a means of survival.

---

1 Psychology Today: https://www.psychologytoday.com/us/basics/compassion-fatigue

Having buried them so deeply, it took me years to re-learn how to experience any emotion outside of the context of cancer and death.

After all the post-death responsibilities were complete, it came time to live on, with a difficult twist: Remember, this all happened at the height of the COVID-19 pandemic. I was left alone and isolated in our house with only our pets as my companions. Being overwhelmed by grief and physical and emotional fatigue, every day was a challenge for me just to get out of bed. The compassion fatigue I felt had also manifested into an unexpected level of mental fatigue. Decision-making of any kind was paralyzing, and carrying out a decision was exhausting. Something as simple as walking the dog took hours of motivational self-talk for me to put on a sweatshirt, grab the leash, and walk out the front door. With all these challenges, I still knew I had to carry on as a widower and somehow recover from the grief of losing Michelle. Every person's journey is unique, but the things I learned as part of my recovery could be summarized in the following lessons:

1. Your physical, mental, and emotional health are just as important as that of the person you're caring for and the people around you. Make your health an equal priority by

    i. Engaging a mental health professional to help you process everything, especially things you've gone numb to.
    ii. Attending to your physical health. Not just with exercise; see a doctor and get a full physical exam. Because of my daily chest pains, I had to make

sure there was no damage to my heart. (Luckily, there was not).

   iii. Quitting toxic habits. I had taken up smoking again as a crutch to manage my stress. It was time to quit for good.

2. Create a team around you.

   i. Instead of trying to be an army of one, be one of an army to help with all aspects of the crisis.
   ii. Though it may not seem like what you need in the moment, in the long run, it will serve you more than you realize.

3. Reframe the difficult time in order to begin the healing.

   i. Not every aspect in my journey was a negative.
   ii. There were and continue to be moments that inspire changes in me as a person and what I do in life going forward.
   iii. I could look back at those positive moments and leverage them to create the roadmap for moving forward with my own journey in life.

4. Overcoming psychic numbness is part of the process of moving through compassion fatigue. Take steps to address this by

i. Becoming aware that you are experiencing psychic numbness.
ii. Not beating yourself up about it.
iii. Engaging a mental health professional and giving yourself permission to be completely vulnerable about your journey.
iv. Giving yourself permission to actually feel the emotions you've been bottling up.

5. Do what you can to keep going and reduce your isolation. Connecting with other people who've gone through similar circumstances can help you express your emotions and feel supported by people who really understand.

i. Put your feet on the floor every morning, and then put one foot in front of the other. Even if you accomplish nothing, at least you are moving forward.
ii. Join a community of people in similar circumstances. For me it was widow(er) support groups; I could learn from their journeys, and they from mine.
iii. Be active in support groups related to your situation if possible. Use these connections as opportunities to learn and grow.

While compassion fatigue is a real thing and is compounded by isolation and grief, it's possible to recover from it and even prevent it. It takes keen attention to noticing the early signs, building a support team for yourself (not just for your loved one) so you can find healthy—instead of toxic—strategies to cope with the crisis, learning to accept that some things are out of your hands, and, most of all, finding ways to give *yourself* compassion so you have fuel in the tank to extend that compassion to your loved one.

Committed

Finding Contentment

A year ago, the path was clear.
I aimed for There and started Here.
So I went forth without delay
to turn my Here to Far Away.
But as I went, each There became
another Here, each one the same.
At every Here I turned around
to see the last Here that I'd found.
I saw that Now had changed to Then
and wanted to go There again.
But this is Now and Here I'll stay,
for There is just too Far Away.

Poppies Along a Path

Jerrald D. Krause, Ph.D.

Jerry Krause fell in love with sociology as a sociology major at UC Berkeley. After five years of teaching and studying in south Louisiana, Jerry returned with Catherine and their growing family to their native California, where Jerry joined the faculty of Humboldt State University. Jerry taught and conducted research there for 34 years. He then taught Aging and Society at Sonoma State University from 2013 to 2019. In order to develop a model for doing empowerment oriented team research, he co-founded and directed the Center for Applied Social Analysis and Education (CASAE) and served as its Director from 1991 until 2005. Before retirement, Jerry worked through CASAE to develop a symbolic interactionist framework for linking theory and research to empowering sociological practice that he calls translational sociology. Since retirement, Jerry's empowerment work has been outside the academy such as with Catherine and Shamana.

Catherine Krause, RN, PHN

Catherine Krause is a speaker, writer and consultant on management and organizational planning. Formerly a Regional Vice President for Community Health for a major health corporation and director of a multi-service home health organization, she has over 30 years' experience and is an expert in management and leadership development. She also worked for two years for Golden Living Centers as a Clinical Liaison and five years as a consultant and owner with Shamana Consulting, Inc. Along with four partners, Catherine also created the Wellness Center in Eureka, where clients could incorporate holistic medical inventions to improve health. Catherine has collaboratively developed and presented with Jerry Krause a four-week series of workshops on EMPOWERED AGING. In these workshops, Catherine shares a holistic model on how to stay empowered while one ages. These workshops help attendees with new ideas on how to support oneself and others as we make difficult decisions that emerge during the aging process.

Catherine Krause, RN, PHN
Jerry Krause, Ph.D.

Lessening Compassion Fatigue Through an Empowerment Approach

When my husband and I decided to have my 90-year-old mother, Bernie, come live with us, we knew we had some work to do. Not just on the house and in day-to-day caregiving duties, but in coming to terms with our own aging process. During those last six years of her life, we learned how to see her as a continuing, growing, empowered person who had more to give and share. We learned how to be a compassionate presence in the midst of sadness and confusion and difficult choices. We learned ways of maintaining our own sense of self and reducing the fatigue that can come from caregiving. And out of it all, we developed a model for empowered aging.

When she moved in with us, our first step was to ensure she had a space that would allow us both privacy, so we reconfigured two of our smaller bedrooms to accommodate an eventual wheelchair, and we dedicated one or our bathrooms for her use only, adding grab bars to the shower. We also hired home care aides to tend to her for a few hours a day so we could continue our work, as a professor and a consultant, and be gone from home.

Having these things in place set some boundaries for us. My motto was "keep my role as daughter and not become only her nurse." I followed the spirit of this motto in advising my clients and friends who were taking care of their family members, and I was their nurse/counselor in my role as home health consultant.

For us, this meant having our own time to work outside the home and then return home and prepare meals and enjoy her company. We were the ones who took her to Mass every Sunday and let her continue to practice her faith in a way she had done for 90 years. We were the ones who prepared family dinners and shared our meals with kids to let her enjoy those who lived locally. We were also the ones who helped her prepare for bed and recited her nightly rosary with her as she had done for many years.

My husband developed an endearing role with her for those bedtime moments, and he labeled himself as "Jason, her night aide." In his words:

One "device" I invented for staying in my son-in-law role with Bernie without becoming a custodial and compassion-fatigued caregiver was to "play-act" the fun pretend role of Jason, a Care Aide at the Charles Avenue Care Home. At Bernie's bedtime every night, I would knock on Bernie's bedroom door, saying, "It's Jason from Patient Care Services!" Bernie would cheerfully reply, "Come in!" I might read something to her or say a decade of the rosary. She was then ready to sleep. After tucking her in and giving her a cup of water, I would say, "Good night! Sleep tight, and don't let the fleas bite!" Then Bernie would recite her well-rehearsed line: "If they do, take a shoe, and crack 'em in two!" After some giggling from Bernie, Jason would then turn out the light and close the door, and Bernie would drift off to sleep.

We worked at keeping our roles as clear as possible and using others, instead of just ourselves, for her personal needs like bathing, showering, morning dressing, and activities of daily living which required the home care aides. I also was able to get my primary care physician to take her into his practice and give her the professional care she needed, and have it covered by her major. So, health care needs were in place, and her emotional, physical, and spiritual needs were all attended to with the help of others. Caregiving is a job one cannot do alone.

During this six-year period, we were able to observe how her experiences from her long and active life had influenced her. She kept a positive attitude and kept making choices for what she needed. Looking back over nearly 100 years of her life, we reflected on the roles she'd had and how those roles changed over time. We later turned this process into a model called Empowered Aging, which we have been teaching in workshops ever since.

To understand how this model works, it is useful to see first how it looks for Bernie's life.

1908 to 1918

Life began in Livermore Valley where her ancestors had settled after arriving from Ireland and pioneering to California. Bernie grew up hearing stories of this new world, which included stories of the Donner Party. During this decade she began tackling early childhood tasks and learning how to be part of a family that included more than just her. She was the youngest of six children, with four brothers and a sister.

1918 to 1928

Between the ages of 10 and 20, Bernie began to transition from childhood to early adulthood. Several significant social "signposts" marked the pathway for her as she moved forward on this journey. The first was graduating from eighth grade. This meant an important shift of perspective. What had been a small, unchanging group of intimate friends now started to become more diversified. Some began to move into larger settings while others remained. She lost contact with some and retained contact with others. Choices began.

Bernie and her sister ("Sissie") shared a continuing close relationship. Their intimate communication continued for many years until Sissie died at age 90. Among the new ways of thinking about herself as a participant in her increasingly diversified social worlds was learning how to be a competitor. Bernie learned to be a great competitive swimmer and committed herself at a young age to swimming across Strawberry Lake, a feat she was proud of and often reminded her children of.

Bernie learned that being a competitor didn't rule out having good, lifelong friendships and being a good, lifelong friend. Friends were a great source of support for her, and she had lots of them.

A very important milestone in Bernie's early adulthood phase was graduation from high school. This was important because very impactful choices had to be made. Two of these choices required leaving home: entering college at San Jose State, and choosing to become a teacher. Those were pretty adventurous choices in those days. Making those choices required empowering commitments—commitments to taking charge of what she wanted to do and where she wanted to be.

1928 to 1938

Between the ages of 20 and 30, Bernie transitioned from early adulthood into adulthood. Two somewhat divergent marker events grounded her passage into adulthood. First, graduation from college led to Bernie taking the role of teacher in a one-room schoolhouse in the faraway town of Snelling, where she lived in a boarding house. Here she began her career in education. Education was a passion for her, a passion that extended to her family, shown by the fact that two of her daughters also entered that career. She would joke that most of her students were taller than she was, and she had to look up to talk to many of them.

The second major adulthood marker event for Bernie during these years was Bernie's marriage, after five years of teaching. It was a risky choice, for an Irish woman to choose an Italian mate along with the complications that went with family approval in both strong cultures. Bernie also began her family, and she dealt well with maintaining her own sense of who she was even with a strong Italian mother-in-law who had clear ideas and presence in her life.

After her marriage in 1936, Bernie chose to continue growing her family, even though it meant putting her teaching career on hold. Teachers were not at that time allowed to teach when pregnant. With five children, her teaching career was on hold.

1938 to 1948

When she was between 30 and 40 years of age, Bernie's major life path roles put motherhood at center stage. Her last child was born in 1945, and Bernie continued to be a caregiver, using her teaching career vision and talents in preparing her kids all to become college bound. Outings, quiet times, and learning to find contentment in simple things were a big part of her life during this period.

1948 to 1958

When she turned 50 years old, Bernie transitioned to midlife roles, in which she refined skills and used expertise that allowed her to return to her teaching. Her career-related activities centered around school. For example, she became PTA President, designed costumes for pageants, and introduced folk dance lessons to her kids' school. Her expertise was focused as a reading specialist.

Bernie's school-focused activities continued despite a busy schedule of activities devoted to friends and family. Her communications and activities were very frequent with friends she maintained for many years. She also maintained a busy schedule of family celebratory activities that marked her marital commitment. She celebrated her 25th wedding anniversary, sharing in the fruits of that commitment and choice. In this midlife period, Bernie also showed that her choice and commitment to her teaching career were alive and well. She returned to classroom teaching after a twenty-year hiatus!

1958 to 1968

When she was 50 to 60 years of age, Bernie's life transitions focused on children beginning to leave home, as they established their own identities as adults in family and work roles. She began to marry kids off. She put energy into going back to being a couple, to figuring out how life works with two again! She also began to enjoy grandparenting, and she celebrated early retirement to enjoy some balance.

1968 to 1978

When Bernie was 60 to 70 years old, she built commitments and choices around making a permanent transition to retirement from teaching. Among the new post-teaching, empty-nest identities she grew into was traveling, such as for her first Hawaiian holiday. Her travels also came to include visiting grandkids, and those grandchildren who lived away insisted that she try new things like riding horses. Bernie also learned to teach grandkids to stop outmoded ways of relating to her, such as learning not to sit on her lap because they had grown too big!

1978 to 1988

When Bernie was in her 70s, she confronted the transitions related to adjusting to the losses of important roles and relationships. She learned to be alone after the early death of her husband, before their 50th wedding anniversary. Friends who had also lost spouses continued as valued support relationships, mentoring Bernie and each other in how to live without one's spouse. Pets were a new addition to her single life, becoming a welcome source of creativity along with newfound art skills. She also now enjoyed the company of grandchildren, who had also now outgrown her in size.

1988 to 1998

When Bernie was 80 to 90 years old, she transitioned to living alone in a new home, while still remaining a vital part of a family that was growing and becoming more geographically dispersed. She was responsible for her own home and continued to give attention to her spiritual health. She continued to participate in family activities and celebrations, which now increasingly included relationships with great-grandchildren. She began also to deal with some health issues. She held herself accountable for staying well, at least for the aspects she could make a difference with.

1998 to 2004

When Bernie was 90 to 96 years of age, Bernie's major role and relationship changes centered around her moving 300 miles away into our home (her daughter and son-in-law) and meeting end-of-life challenges. She fell and broke her hip and was unable to care for herself independently. She chose to move out of her hometown where she had lived for 90 years. With her new living situation as a "base of action," she remained engaged in family activities, including practicing and performing her dance with her grandson at his wedding and then greeting more great-grandchildren. She celebrated her 95th birthday in 2003, a year before she died in 2004 at 96 years of age.

Moving to an Empowered Aging Model Building from Past Learned Traits

It is with this decade reflection exercise that we began to unconsciously identify the traits she had acquired from these life experiences before and after we cared for her. We began to encourage her to translate her past capacities to new ones that would be more helpful to her in her new role and place. We wanted to encourage her to stay empowered and be in charge of her changing world, and not simply turn her power over to others.

The life experiences we identified, and the strengths that Bernie learned from them over her many years, we categorized as **Accountability, Authority, Choices, Influence, and Knowledge.**

Over the time we cared for Bernie, we watched those strengths transform to a higher level that would help her function in her new role. We observed that **Accountability** shifted to **Self-Awareness**, **Authority** shifted to **Groundedness, Choice Making** shifted to **Commitments**, **Influence** shifted to **Compassion,** and **Knowledge** shifted to **Wisdom**.

By conceptualizing Bernie's strengths in this way, we realized we could assist her in staying empowered and not giving up the value she had to contribute to the world. I had witnessed so many situations in my nursing career where elders were told what to do and were given very little input on how they wanted to continue to contribute. What follows is our description of an empowered aging model and an explanation of its value when caregiving, to lessen or avoid compassion fatigue. The following model and explanation are based on the idea that to empower others is to empower yourself.

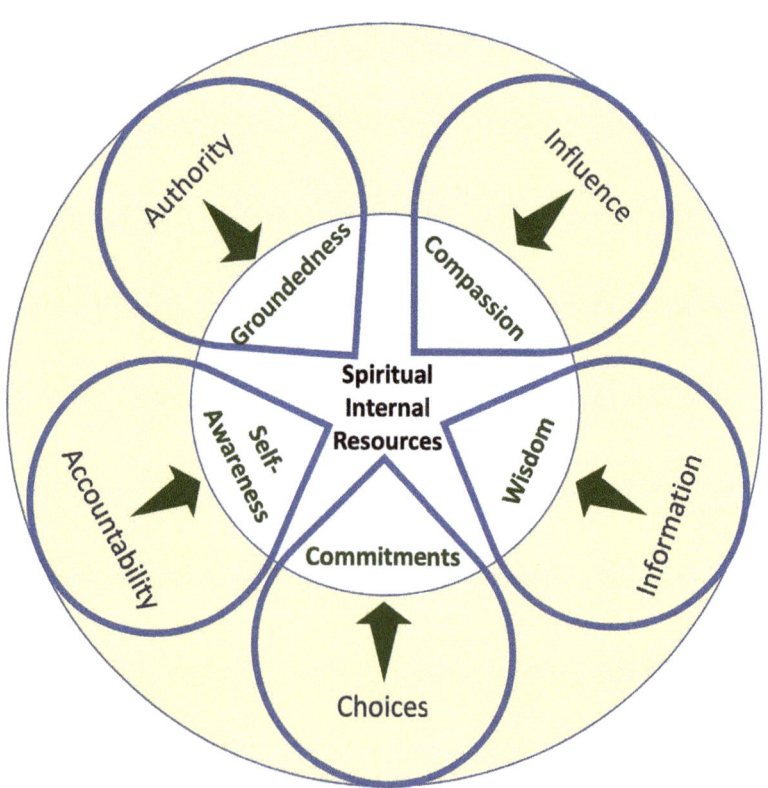

Accountability to Self-Discovery

Accountability

This includes how we take responsibility for our successes and failures by keeping track of them. It involves the schedules and deadlines we set for ourselves as well as the progress we make in meeting them. We frequently set goals or make plans and then hold ourselves responsible for achieving them. We use tools to assist us and structures such as agreements, negotiations, and progress markers. We learn to evaluate our own value as we meet those deadlines, goals, and achievements.

Moving from Accountability to Self-Discovery

Helping Bernie tell her past stories of accountability and reinforcing her learnings were key to her moving to greater self-awareness. This began the process of letting go of who she was in the past and beginning the definition of who she was now. For example, telling stories of how she once took care of five kids, taught at the same time, and managed a busy schedule gave her a sense of accomplishment. Now she was being cared for and was trying to redefine her contributions as a 90 year old. In the past she used to jump out of bed to start her day. Now, she needed assistance as she woke up and got dressed.

It's a question of how one transforms their old accountability skills learned in the past into a new way of acting that includes being cared for by others. Self-acceptance of what one can do now is a great part of learned self-awareness.

Self-awareness grows by asking oneself several questions and reflecting on one's role: How can I now act with others who are interested in assisting me, and how do I, in turn, give what I have back? The things I have done and learned can be shared, and my experiences can be of help to others. These insights can be a source of mentoring for those around me, especially for younger generations.

As I age, I can see more clearly the importance of being myself and acknowledging what others need, and I can hold a bigger picture as a result. What did I learn from the times I met or failed my past goals? What did I contribute when I met those goals?

The answers to these questions helped Bernie look at what she was now doing and gave her some new clues on how to cope and evolve. She began to reflect on past accomplishments by remembering how accountability served her and by using them as steps to new self-awareness. In learning to walk with a walker after her broken hip, she reflected on her great swim across Strawberry Lake and the endurance she had as a means to walk further each day. The more self-reflective she was, the better she saw who she was now and saw what she could offer to others. She stayed empowered and made progress by not giving away what she was responsible for in regaining her strength and health.

Questions that may help us define ways we have been accountable include the following:

- How do I use the strengths I have developed in being accountable to move forward with greater self-awareness now?

- What forms of accountability from my past can I utilize to increase my self-awareness?
- What patterns of accountability have I practiced over the years?
- How does being accountable for my own progress move me to a stronger sense of self?

Authority to Groundedness

Authority

We possess authority when our views are put to use by others to make decisions and change behavior. Authority helps others move forward. We may struggle with rules or external values imposed on us. Those authorities are teaching us. In our career or professional path, we play by the rules set by the organization, and in parenting we follow ideas learned from experts. We choose guides in life who share our values. Different experts or authorities influence us, and then we develop our own means of being the authority so we can be sought out by others to assist in their development. In most cases, this exterior authority we develop helps us to succeed.

Moving from Authority to Groundedness

Our growing self-knowledge as we age can bring us newfound inner authority that allows us to accept our new place and new roles that present in our lives. And in some cases, to even welcome new people into them. Thoughts such as *I am glad to be me and grateful to be where I am* are simple statements to reflect what groundedness means. As we age in our new surroundings, we begin to feel rooted. We create a place where we can stand firmly and take a deeper look at the challenges we face, and with our learnings of the past turn them into opportunities. It is a time of trusting our past experiences and our inner self-knowledge, and testing them with how it all fits. Our experiences of using our authority for power now are turned inward.

My husband and I were lucky to be able to give Bernie her own space, which included her bedroom and a sitting TV room and her bathroom. Being able to move some of her furniture into the space helped her feel grounded in new surroundings. She kept in charge of her space with assistance, but it definitely was *her* space.

She also experienced a lot of loss during this time, and sometimes it created great loneliness. Using her inner authority could be very difficult when many of the friends she had were dying and no longer available to her. It was hard to listen to her own advice and recall when she experienced being an authority without their validation. Bernie used the foundational work of the outer authority to transform it into the inner authority. She began to build new habits for herself and let go of those things that were not there anymore. She accepted the neighbor who came to pray her rosary with her every Friday and began to see her as a new friend. When we attended weekly Mass, she was open to exploring relationships with those at church who wanted to share with her.

Bernie generated some new rules in this uncharted place where she found herself. With the assistance of a caregiver each day she was still in charge of deciding her wake up time, her meal time, her bathing time, and her bed time. She kept her authority over those things to help her stay grounded with where she was now. She was listened to for the things she needed to stay in charge of as she gave up the things she no longer could handle. She kept in touch with her children on a regular basis and sent them notes about what she was doing. She renewed her interest in painting.

She found new ways of being in a world that had changed. She felt grounded in herself and continued to make new things happen. For her it also meant learning to use a walker to prevent falls so that she could keep moving. She gave up two-mile walks but continued to exercise and was swimming with her granddaughter once a week. She continued moving from room to room and enjoying the back patio, but it took a walker and assistance which she accepted as her new way of being.

Some questions that may help us at this stage of change are as follows:

- Who do I see as in charge of, or who has authority over my aging?
- How do I get my thoughts and ideas supported, listened to, and accepted?
- Who do I go to for advice?
- Who do I know who is in charge?
- Who comes to me for decisions?
- What parts of my life do I absolutely want to control?
- What am I ready to let go of?
- How am I using the authority practice I once had to help myself? To help others?

Choices to Commitments

Choices

We make choices throughout our lives that result in consequences. We are given options to make decisions to either enrich or deplete our lives. They may serve us to give us more energy or serve as barriers to our goals. We may push against choices and become resistant in our actions. In our early life we are presented with many choices and time to make them.

Moving from Choices to Commitments

As we age, we are presented with fewer choices and less time. We therefore need to prioritize and focus on the things that matter most to us. We deal with all the changes that come and begin to commit to a few important things rather than deal with the multitude of choices we had before. Commitment allows us to focus our energy on a few choices rather than the many we had in the past. These limits help us understand the importance of choice, and committing to a few allows us more satisfaction in the ones we have.

Giving Bernie choices at the beginning of the move so she could visualize the changes ahead and be prepared to deal with each of them made a difference to her commitment. After her decision to move was made, she committed to a plan and began working on how to live fully in her new environment. She had choice in picking her caregivers. She had choice in when to have her meals, and when to arise and go to bed at night. We and other caregivers avoided putting her in situations that made her feel disempowered.

Questions that may help in making new commitments include taking a look at the beliefs we hold and reflecting on the concepts or values that guide our decisions.

- What has been my code of behavior, and how has it impacted my life?
- What values drive me now? Are they different from the values I held in the past?
- How am I being a participant in the process of my aging? Am I just letting it happen? What am I doing to keep myself empowered as I age?
- How am I enlisting others to support and create a positive aging process to let me fulfill my commitments?
- What are the commitments I am prioritizing for myself to live the life I want to be living?
- What past choices have influenced who I am now? Are they still part of my present commitments?

Knowledge to Wisdom

Knowledge

We acquire much information as we age. It comes in various forms and from various places. We pride ourselves on learning and collecting certificates or degrees in various subjects. We use this knowledge and share it with others.

Moving from Knowledge to Wisdom

When we begin to translate our knowledge into discernment and learning, we call that wisdom. We take on a new role as the thinker or philosopher and share a bigger perspective that leads to the benefit of knowing those facts. Wisdom takes a long view and is more of a reflective fact-telling. It forces us to tell the truth about what we have seen, and what we have personally been through, and to share what it means with another. It is more than just the facts of what happened. It involves sharing what happened so that another can learn from it. We move from simple information to meaningful impact. The fact could be the knowledge that I turned 30, but the wisdom behind that fact involves what happened to me as a result. Wisdom is reflected in the words of the song "I Can See Clearly Now" and connects how all the pieces fit together in life. If I take a trip and learn facts about a country, that is knowledge. When I tell what happened to me personally as a result of the travel, that becomes wisdom.

Bernie shared her life stories and always included what she had learned from the experience. This kept the grandkids interested in areas they were dealing with in their own lives. In sharing her story of meeting her husband and the issues of blending two different cultures, hearing of the impacts that had on her was very helpful to them. Stories of her career as a teacher in a one-room school house brought the wisdom of how to deal with people from many different backgrounds.

Questions that may help one move from knowledge to wisdom include the following:

- Where do I now get my information?
- How am I using my listening skills?
- Am I keeping current on technical, professional, and political changes and interpreting them with my learned skills?
- Do I share my personal expertise with others?
- What are my present sources of information?
- How am I feeling the impact of what I am learning now?
- Am I sharing my learnings? With whom?
- How am I gaining knowledge that will assist me in staying empowered as I age?

Influence to Compassion

Influence

Influence involves how we affect each other. How can we sway another to change their mind or to do what we want? We have had positions of power that enabled our influence in family, work, or community. Influence involves an element of competition and also may include a sense of control.

Moving from Influence to Compassion

With compassion, we move to a place of emptying ourselves, not filling ourselves. We reach out to others rather than wait for them to reach out to us. Compassion has a more communal quality than an individual one. It is a movement from *me* to *we*. As we age, we begin to lose some of the influences we have carried. We lose some physical strength and begin to move more slowly. We find ourselves in situations where we have less value and begin to deal with a loss of influence. The shift to compassion from influence can give us a new and different focus. We can begin to see the needs of others more and not only worry about our own needs. When we reach out to assist others, we can help ourselves by developing relationships of equality. We can share our own struggles along with their struggles and begin to see what we have in common. We can assist each other with those needs. A new cooperative relationship can grow and bring us new calm and peace. Living with a compassionate presence can lead us on a new path in making the transition to elder.

Bernie had valued many friendships during her long life, and she was valued by her friends. When she moved in with us, she had a variety of new people to meet. She made an effort to learn about them and become a listener to their stories. She would reach out to them with support and comfort. She was comfortable with my husband's professor colleagues who visited as well as home care aides who were with her daily. She shared her compassionate ear with them and was present to the issues they talked about. Once again, she let other people into her life and valued their contact.

Questions that may help us evolve in this area include:

- How am I continuing to make and increase my relationships with others?
- Do I nurture and sustain relationships with a wide range of people?
- How am I choosing my friends and making allies?

- How do I resolve conflicts?
- Do I feel creative in what I am doing?
- Do I feel passion and compassion in my daily life?
- How do I use the graces I have within me to produce effects for others?
- Am I listening with a competitive or compassionate ear?

Finding New Ways of Being

We found that caring for another required us to find new ways of being in order to help us maintain our compassionate presence. Our empowerment model of transforming past experiences to a higher level gave us some new ideas on how to stay empowered and keep our patient empowered, too. We found that sharing the model in workshops with others—either older themselves, or caregivers caring for elders—also proved helpful.

We have found that in order to be successful in caring for an older person, it was crucial to get in touch with our own ideas about aging. We chose to see aging in a strength-based way. This connection allowed us to begin to deal with our own mortality (or illusion of immortality) and assist us in compassionate caring. This change required us to understand the meaning of compassion and put it into action. It is more than being kind or having pity.

The changes that Bernie went through during those six years, and that we went through as caregivers, were transitions from external influence to an internal one. We experienced a shift from *getting* to *giving*, and that changed both our focus and how we saw ourselves.

The areas we shared on our empowerment wheel are the shifts we went through that allowed us to sustain a compassionate mode and to lessen fatigue. The key, we believe, to reducing compassion fatigue is learning to see and to activate the internal (spiritual) resources when giving care and receiving care. Empowering self awareness created groundedness and led to commitments and wisdom that resulted in sustained compassion.

Sailing Onward

www.ingramcontent.com/pod-product-compliance
Lightning Source LLC
LaVergne TN
LVHW072336080526
838199LV00121B/601/J